DREAM
DOER

DREAM
DOER

Dream Building Secrets
from the Life of Noah

PAUL E. TSIKA

DESTINY IMAGE® PUBLISHERS, INC.

P.O. Box 310, Shippensburg, PA 17257-0310

"Promoting Inspired Lives."

This book and all other Destiny Image and Destiny Image Fiction books are available at Christian bookstores and distributors worldwide.

For more information on foreign distributors, call 717-532-3040.

Reach us on the Internet: www.destinyimage.com.

HC ISBN: 978-0-7684-6382-8

For Worldwide Distribution, Printed in the U.S.A.

1 2 3 4 5 6 7 8 / 26 25 24 23 22

DEDICATION

MR. ANGELO TSIKA
Music Director

I learned to dream as a kid by watching Saturday morning serials on black and white TV. I watched shows like *Roy Rogers, Gene Autry, Hopalong Cassidy, The Lone Ranger and Tonto, The Red Rider, Superman* and *Rocket Man*. My favorite, though, was *This Is Your Life*. I was glued to the TV to witness some person who would be spotlighted for his wonderful contribution to life. I was mesmerized by what I saw: various individuals shared their account of the spotlighted person's past accomplishments.

I would lay in bed at night and dream about doing something great with my life. A wonderful thing about dreaming is that no one can steal your dream, unless you allow them to. Also, in a dream, no obstacles, barriers or challenges are too great that you can't just blow by them confidently.

When I was a teenager, I read an article my Dad wrote entitled "Dreams Do Come True." Dad was an immigrant from Albania and saw his dream come true; he attained American citizenship (March 17, 1937), graduated from the Boston Conservatory of Music, and married my mom, who was voted the "best looking" in her class at Stearns High School in Millinocket, Maine. Dad's article was published in *Reader's Digest* and had a lot of great reviews.

My father and I did not have a close relationship. The older I got the more I began to understand that a lot of the distance between us was due to his lack of relationship with his dad. It is sad to think that so many in that generation went through the same grief.

My father, however, cared about us well in the way he could, the way he knew how. He put food on the table, a roof over our heads, and clothes on our backs. He always provided for his family. In spite of some pain, I do have great memories of childhood.

So I'd like to dedicate this book on dreaming to a man that taught me by his actions and hard work that dreams do come true: Angelo D. Tsika (1914-1986).

My father lived his dream and because of the wonderful love of God, I am living mine. Thank you, dear Lord Jesus.

So, to all Dreamers everywhere, this is for you as well.

ACKNOWLEDGMENTS

Billie Kaye Tsika—Her gift is the love, support and freedom she gives me every day to write. Her insightfulness and writing skills have always helped me with my manuscripts. I love her more today than yesterday. Sounds like a song but one that's true in our life.

Destiny Image—Our partnership in publishing our works has always been a wonderful experience. I'm thankful for their heart to always do it right for the authors under their banner.

Dr. J. Tod Zeiger—Who has always been able to take my notes, thoughts, and ramblings and make them coherent. His availability as a friend, advisor and co-laborer has made my life an easy transition from my manuscripts to readable books.

Thomas J. Tsika—Thom has been the CFO of our ministry for over 17 years. Without his counsel, guidance and input I would be that ball lost in tall weeds. He has great wisdom, insight and direction for all we do at the ranch. Like I've always said, "he may be wrong, but he's never in doubt."

Gretchen Ann (Tsika) Rush—She has been invaluable with proofreading and correcting all of my books. Her strength of character during these days since Mark's passing has been inspiring.

My Family—They are my cheering section, every one of them. Their love and support have added such great value to my life. They all inspire, and spur me on to new horizons. My family has made my life full, and I love them all.

CONTENTS

PREFACE

Are you a dreamer? Do you imagine or visualize secret aspirations? This book is about dreamers, like you. But, it is especially about *doing* in order to see those dreams come true. Dreaming and *doing* go hand in hand, like faith and works. One supports the other and together they make dreams a reality. I won't bore you with a lot of stories and illustrations here. I simply want you to dive into my most recent book, and I believe my best yet. Read, underline, think, move slowly, enjoy, and then get up and act upon what you've read.

Noah's life is a perfect example of a man standing alone who heard from God, dreamed of pleasing Him and got the job done. His life's work stands as a memorial for the seemingly impossible.

I've always been a big dreamer. Even as a lonely child growing up in Maine, I had big dreams to do something monumental with my life. I wanted to be the hero of my own story. But somewhere along the line, I realized that dreaming, when not followed up by hard work, will turn into a nightmare. And, in 1971, I met the real hero of my story and will be forever grateful for His love and grace that has enabled me to be a doer and not just a dreamer. That hero is none other than the Lord Jesus Christ—who changed my life forever!

The Bible tells us in the book of Acts how the early disciples worked, witnessed, prayed, studied, ministered, denied themselves, worshiped, sang, served God. The author of the book of Acts declared, *"and they continued steadfastly."* Those four words stopped me in my tracks; *"and they continued steadfastly"* (Acts 2:42). The disciples always did the much more that made the early church a success and their dream of establishing the gospel reach the world. From those four words, I derived the following acrostic that I believe is the key to a dream becoming successful:

Doing

Repeatedly

Essentials

And

More...

In order to become a DREAM DOER you must continue steadfastly in those principles that made you successful in the beginning, in your Christian life, in your marriage, in your business, or any relationship.

PASTOR PAUL E. TSIKA

1

THE CARPE DIEM EFFECT

(Don't Miss the Boat)

Tomorrow is not promised and the past cannot be changed therefore live each day to the fullest and know that every new day is a blessing.

—NISHAN PANWAR[1]

Noah did everything just as God commanded him.

—GENESIS 6:22

Noah's story, the flood, and the destruction and restoration of the human race, have been discussed, re-told, and hashed out by philosophers, preachers, and critics for centuries. Everyone has an opinion as to whether the story of the great flood took place. My purpose is not to debate the issue. As for me, I believe the Biblical account—and you can feel free to form your own opinion.

My goal is to use Noah's story as a "jumping off" point to highlight key lessons that can benefit anyone who aspires to reach a new level of leadership. Learning lessons of successful leadership are all around us if we will pay attention. And that includes a man who took on the task of building the world's biggest boat [at that time].

For the sake of time and space (and undue repetition), let me offer a quick overview of the challenges Noah and his family faced.

Eleven Facts About Noah's Ark

1. According to Bible scholars, Noah was born in 2928 B.C. and was approximately 480 years old when God asked him to build a boat that would save the animals and his family.

2. God determined to wipe out the human race because of all of their evil (Genesis 6:5-7).

3. God issued the order that mankind had one hundred years to clean up their act, or it was over (Genesis 6:3).

4. According to the Bible, Noah was a man of faith who found favor in the eyes of God (Hebrews 11:5-7; Genesis 6:9).

5. Noah not only built the largest ship up to that time but "it would be the largest sailing vessel man would construct until around the 1800's A.D.! It displaced (at a draught of 15 cubits) more than 22,000 tons of water. God told Noah to make a ship with over 101,000 square feet (9,383 square meters) of floor space. Because it was built on the 1:6 ratio (50 cubits: 300 cubits) which modern naval architecture reveals is the most stable for ocean-going vessels, it would be almost impossible to turn the ship over!"[2]

6. Noah proves you are never too old to build, being six hundred years old when the Ark set sail.

7. Noah and his team took over one hundred years to build the Ark.

8. The Ark had no destination. Its sole purpose was to float, and, therefore, had no steering wheel.

9. Rain and "floodgates of the heavens were opened" for forty days and forty nights. According to the Bible, the water was 15 cubits high, or about 23 feet.

10. Noah and his family (wife, sons, and sons' wives) were stuck on the Ark for one year and ten days.

11. After coming off the Ark, God showed a rainbow as a sign of His covenant (promise) for all mankind that He would never flood the Earth again.

There's so much more about the Ark and its relation to leadership in the modern era that will be discovered in the coming chapters.

NOAH HAD A CARPE DIEM MOMENT

Carpe diem is a Latin phrase that has been popularized in the last few decades, especially in books, movies, and politics. The general definition is "seizing the opportunity, or seizing the day."

> Seize the opportunity to grow, learn, and adjust. Look for an opportunity behind every door. Do not be afraid of results or outcomes. Do not fear consequences. Take risks and take chances if you want to see change. Opportunity holds the key to success and

<u>fulfillment.</u> If you don't seize every opportunity, how will you know that you didn't miss the ticket to your future?[3]

You might remember a movie released in 1989 starring Robin Williams, who played an English teacher, John Keating, at a boy's prep school. The film was entitled *Dead Poets Society.* There was one scene in the movie in which Keating wanted to inspire his students; he stood them in front of a trophy case and explained the weightiness of Carpe Diem:

> Gather ye rosebuds while ye may. The Latin term for that sentiment is Carpe Diem. Now, who knows what that means? Carpe Diem. That's "seize the day." Gather ye rosebuds while ye may. Why does the writer use these lines? Because we are food for the worms, lads. Because believe it or not, each and every one of us in this room is one day going to stop breathing, turn cold, and die.
>
> Now I would like you to step forward over here and peruse some of the faces from the past. You have walked past them many times. I don't think you've really looked at them. They're not very different from you, are they? Same haircuts. Full of hormones, just like you. Invincible, just like you feel. The world is their oyster. They believe they're destined for great things, just like many of you. Their eyes are full of hope, just like you. Did they wait until it was too late to make from their lives even one iota of what they were capable of?

Because you see, gentlemen, these boys are now fertilizing daffodils. But if you listen real close, you can hear them whisper their legacy to you. Go on, Lean in. Listen. Do you hear it? (whispers) Carpe. (whispers again) Carpe. Carpe diem. Seize the day, boys, make your lives extraordinary.

This adrenaline-pumping speech explains the literal and philosophical meaning behind carpe diem. Carpe diem is a war-cry. Carpe diem invokes the sleeping giant within you. It urges you to shed your inhibitions, pluck some courage, and grab every opportunity that comes your way. Carpe diem is the best way to say, "You only live once."[4]

How does the *carpe diem effect* apply to the story of Noah?

Quite simply, Noah had to make a decision. He did not have the option to "mull it over" or to consult with his friends. His decision would affect the rest of his life and the lives of his family. The future of mankind depended on what he would do. What would have happened if he had not taken action when he heard the Word of the Lord?

No small thing to ponder you say...

I would say you are correct!

THE CRUCIAL QUESTION: What did Noah do when the door of opportunity opened, and he had to decide—"Will I choose to do as God commanded?" and "Will I take the risk of doing something that's never been done—build the world's largest boat...or not?" There was a tipping point when this crazy plan could have gone either way—he could have said, "No! I'm not going to spend my time building a boat and wait for something to happen that's never happened before, namely rain."

Noah said yes, and it is recorded that Noah... *"did everything just as God commanded him..."* (Genesis 6:22).

And, the rest, as they say, is history!

THE LAW OF OPPORTUNITY IS STILL IN EFFECT

Oftentimes, behind difficult or challenging circumstances lie an opportunity for growth or change—if we choose to take it on. Many times we are forced to seek or cling to the comfort, company, direction, wisdom or help of our loving Father God. All the benefits or opportunities of going through a storm are rarely known before you come out the other side of a storm and look back.

William Douglas and Teiseira Reubens, in their book *The Twenty Five Laws of Biblical Success,* purports the law of opportunity states: "everyone at some point will have an opportunity to get ahead in life."[5] Although Jesus does not give a parallel statement about such a law, scripture does say that we have a choice between choosing obedience which will bring blessings and life or curses which brings destruction (Deuteronomy 30:19). Which sounds like success to you?

That doesn't mean everyone will view opportunities the same way or achieve the same results. Nor does it mean everyone will rise to the same level of success, but what it means is the door of blessings (opportunities) will open for those willing to obey God even if it means we take a risk to attempt something we have never done before.

Michael Levine observed:

> I'm sure we can all agree that opportunity is never a lengthy visitor; in fact, it is often downright fleeting. The elements that come together to create any new enterprise, whether grand or modest, are in constant flux; so, the "liquid circumstances" that make up an opportunity one moment may well be radically altered or even evaporate altogether by the next. Therefore, we must be prepared, willing, and available to seize the opportunity the moment it comes calling.[6]

In another passage of Scripture, Jesus talked about two men who built houses, and He illustrates what the law of opportunity looks like. Jesus said:

> *Therefore everyone who hears these words of mine and puts them into practice is like a wise man who built his house on the rock. The rain came down, the streams rose, and the winds blew and beat against that house; yet it did not fall, because it had its foundation on the rock. But everyone who hears these words of mine and does not put them into practice is like a foolish man who built his house on sand. The rain came down, the streams rose, and the winds blew and beat against that house, and it fell with a great crash* (Matthew 7:24-27).

- Both, the wise man and the foolish man had the same opportunity to build on a solid foundation.
- One chose to build his house on "the rock" while the foolish man chose to build his house on sand.

Foundation

(The "rock" referred to here are the wise teachings of Christ.)

- Both houses looked the same on the outside. A casual observer would not be able to see what was underneath (the foundation).
- Both men faced the same test (a terrible storm).
- It took a storm to reveal what could not be seen with the natural eye.

WHAT CAN WE LEARN?

When OPPORTUNITY knocks on our door, it is sometimes dressed like a crisis. President J.F. Kennedy once remarked that "When written in Chinese, the word 'crisis' is composed of two characters. One represents danger, and the other represents opportunity." Every crisis is, at the same time, an opportunity. Unexpected difficulties often cause crises. All of us have problems. Many of us will face crises. How do you respond to a time of trouble, danger, or unexpected difficulties in your personal life? How do we react to unforeseen challenges in the church or our nation? What do we do when we are "at [our] wits' end"? (Psalm 107:27). What do we do when the "truth of the gospel" is at stake? (Galatians 2:5). How do we respond to a black day in our lives? (Isaiah 37:3, MSG).[7]

All of us are going to face storms no matter what we do to wish or pray them away. You see, both the wise man and the foolish man in the parable in the Matthew 7 had the opportunity to make sure that they would be prepared when the storms came. Likewise, no matter what we do to wish them away or pray them away, all of us are going to face storms. Whether it is a financial storm, a death in the family, a sudden loss of a job, or a pandemic of global proportions—storms will find all of us, storms are going to come. That's not the issue. The issue is, what will we do about them when they show up? Do we hide in our basements, or do we *persevere* and face them as an opportunity? Can we follow the wisdom of James, *"Consider it pure joy, my brothers and sisters, whenever you face trials of many kinds, because you know that the testing of your faith produces perseverance. Let perseverance finish its work so that you may be mature and complete, not lacking anything"* (James 1:2-4)?

It is not enough to know that the door of opportunity is open; we must be willing to take advantage and "seize the day." Noah faced aliteral storm about to burst on the Earth that would wipe out all life. On the flip side of the crisis was the opportunity to save his family and experience God's renewed covenant with him. In the midst of the crisis, Noah did not hesitate to take the opportunity God set before him, and we must follow his lead.

As leaders, we must learn when to seize an opportunity and take a risk to change what we are doing. Change can be an opportunity, provision, or rescue from a path that is no longer working. Change can set a new and different course of action. While it's true that some doors open more widely than others, we must resist fear of failure which would paralyze our efforts to capture the opportunity staring us in the face.

Happiness, as many say, is not a matter of circumstances but of how you deal with the circumstances you are given. In life, you will be called to react to a number of things—some are foreseeable while others are unpredictable. The best you can do is learn how to seize the opportunities. Hence, your success doesn't depend on the number of chances you get but on the ones you take.[8]

BUT...

I SEE AN ELEPHANT IN THE ROOM— AND HIS NAME IS CHANGE!

Everything about Noah's life was about to change. I find no record where he resisted or even complained. He just obeyed—period! A storm of "Biblical proportions" was on the way, and if Noah didn't step up to the plate and allow change to take place, he would drown like the rest of the world.

What about us? Every action we take will always have the accompanying risk that is equal to the amount of change we are willing to endure.

Don't wait. The time will never be just right.
—**NAPOLEON HILL**[9]

Can there be any doubt that Noah's family (and even Noah himself) was filled with anxiety about what God asked him to do? And yet Noah moved ahead with the knowledge that what God had called him to do was the right thing, no matter how much fear was involved. There are times in our lives when we are challenged to move out of our comfort zone and trust that God knows better than we do. Keep in mind, if we resist change, we may lose something good. But, if we are willing to allow transformation to take place, we will possibly gain something better. It's always about a willingness to take a risk, and that is the scary part. An old Spanish proverb says, *"A wise man changes his mind, a fool never will."*

MY TOP FIVE REASONS WHY WE ARE SO RESISTANT TO CHANGE

1. *It Wasn't My Idea.*

When people don't feel like change is their idea, they will probably oppose the suggestion. The best way to cut down on resistance is to allow those who will be affected by the changes to have input into the process.

2. *I Can't See What's Ahead!*

I heard someone say that people are more comfortable with the old problems than with new solutions—I agree with that statement one hundred percent! I have found that some people are open to change as long as it doesn't cost them anything. Help people to envision the outcomes. Communicate the next steps you will be taking so they have time to adjust and ask questions. Changing the way we do things can produce the same fear as a ship sailing into uncharted waters; ships were not built to stay in port but for sailing on the open sea—so are we!

3. *I Like the Old Way Better.*

When change is introduced, it is often followed by the well-worn phrase "But, we've never done it that way before." The default position of many is going back to what we have been comfortable doing—instead of trying something new. Doing the same old thing is comfortable, but is not always progressive.

4. I Didn't Know THIS Was Coming.

The THIS in that statement refers to any new idea, or any new change that is introduced. Rosabeth Moss Kanter, writing in the Harvard Business Review, said, *"Decisions imposed on people suddenly, with no time to get used to the idea or prepare for the consequences, are generally resisted. It's always easier to say No than to say Yes."*[10] She's right, and I have seen that attitude up close and personal.

5. Fear of Failure.

A change was coming to Noah's life. He didn't back up or resist, but he moved ahead with the God-given plan. He had never undertaken anything close to what was required of him, but it was apparent that Noah had a can-do attitude that allowed him to be successful.

It was author James Baldwin who said, "Not everything that is faced can be changed. But nothing can be changed until it is faced. …Most of us are about as eager to change as we were to be born and go through our changes in a similar state of shock."[11]

ONE MORE THOUGHT…

What will you do when your carpe diem moment arrives? Will you face it and walk through the door of opportunity, or run the other way? Failure to seize the day will not only produce a certain amount of fear and anxiety, but I can guarantee it will also produce the same outcome—nothing! I recently read a statement that sums up the entire matter:

When the door of opportunity opens, follow it. Don't spend your time trying to beat down doors that won't budge. So, don't ignore the open doors while trying to kick in the closed ones. It's called "following the favor!"

—AUTHOR IS UNKNOWN

ENDNOTES

1. https://www.wiseoldsayings.com/carpe-diemquotes/ #ixzz6VOM6jUYV accessed August 1, 2020.

2. https://www.biblestudy.org/question/how-long-did-it-take-noah-to -build-ark.html accessed August 1, 2020.

3. http://www.plazacollege.edu/the-beneficial-meaning-behind-carpe -diem/;accessed August 1, 2020.

4. https://www.thoughtco.com/inspiring-quotes-carpe-diem-2831933 accessed November 2, 2020.

5. William Douglas and Rubens Teixeira, *The 25 Biblical Laws of Success* (Grand Rapids, MI: Baker Books, 2017), 17.

6. Michael Levine, *7 Life Lessons from Noah's Ark* (Berkeley, CA: Celestial Arts Publishing, 2003) 25-26.

7. https://www.bibleinoneyear.org/bioy/commentary/3027 accessed September 2, 2020.

8. William Douglas and Rubens Teixeira, *The 25 Biblical Laws of Success* (Grand Rapids, MI: Baker Books, 2017), 18.

9. https://www.wiseoldsayings.com/carpe-diem-quotes/ #ixzz6VOMS0f2s; accessed August 2, 2020.

10. Rosabeth Moss Kanter, "Ten Reasons People Resist Change," https:// hbr.org/2012/09/ten-reasons-people-resist-chang accessed September 20, 2020.

11. James Baldwin in "As Much Truth as One Can Bear" in *The New York Times* Book Review (14 January 1962); as quoted in Wisdom for the Soul: Five Millennia of Prescriptions for Spiritual Healing (2006) by Larry Chang, p. 114 https://en.wikiquote.org/wiki/Change accessed September 20, 2020.

2

YOU BETTER KNOW THE 'WHY'

(Fight Like You're the Third Monkey in Line!)

It's not enough to have lived. We should be determined to live for something.

—WINSTON S. CHURCHILL[1]

The Lord then said to Noah, "Go into the ark, you and your whole family, because I have found you righteous in this generation."

—GENESIS 7:1

God had chosen Noah for a special purpose—Noah and his family would be the remnant to whom God would confirm His covenant. We have to ask ourselves, why did God choose Noah and why was Noah so ready to follow God's commands? Scripture is clear why: *"Noah was a righteous man, the only blameless man on the earth*

17

at that time and he [Noah] *walked in close fellowship with God"* (Gen. 6:9, NLT). God and Noah had close fellowship. They knew one another and were fellowshipping—talking and spending time together. They trusted one another and were unified. Noah knew God's heart and had faith that God would keep His covenant. God knew Noah's devotion and "righteous ways" and that Noah would be obedient to Him. They knew each other—they spent time together—they were present with one another. Noah's overarching purpose was to be with God, spend time and be present with Him.

This seeking God's presence was not an anomaly among our great forefather-leaders. Adam walked with God (Gen. 3:8), *"Enoch walked faithfully with God"* (Gen. 5:22); *"the Lord was with Joseph"* (Gen 39:2); Abraham walked with God (Gen. 17); Moses walked with God (Exod. 33:15-17); David lived in the presence of God. *"My hearts says of you, 'Seek his face!' Your face, Lord, I will seek"* (Psalm 27:8). Jesus Himself sought time to be in the presence of God even when great miracles were afoot. "Let us go to a quiet place," He told the disciples when they were clamoring to be among the crowds (Mark 6:29). Hebrews 11 affirms the faith of a parade of trusting people who entered into the presence of God fully trusting Him, fully believing in His promises—even before those promises were fulfilled. It's called faith. The number one most important purpose we have in order to be successful is to live in the presence of God and to fellowship with Him. Because Noah and these other faith-leaders fellowshipped and knew God, they could trust His heart, His promises, His provision, and His plans—they had faith that what God promised would be.

Noah had a purpose.

His purpose fueled his passion.

His purpose and passion led him to complete a seemingly impossible job.

It all started with his WHYs.

Although Noah had no earthly mentor to give him "leadership advice" on what to do, the Scripture records that Noah obeyed God. The first step in Noah's success is that he fellowshipped with God. The second step is he did everything that was asked of him—he obeyed God. "*Noah did everything just as God commanded him*" (Genesis 6:22). "*And Noah did all that the Lord commanded him*" (Genesis 7:5).

Being purposed of God and being obedient are intertwined. Listening to and obeying are the same word in Hebrew—*Shema*. There is no space between hearing God and obeying. When one hears God, he obeys God. If your ultimate purpose is to walk with God, i.e. live in the presence of God, then it follows that your ultimate purpose is to obey Him. The first article of Westminster's small catechism is "What Is Man's Purpose?" The answer is: To know the Lord and to enjoy His presence forever. Listen to what the Lord clearly tells the nation of Israel through Moses in Deuteronomy about our choices to obey God:.

> *Today I have given you the choice between life and death, between blessings and curses. Now I call on heaven and earth to witness the choices you make to obey God. Oh, that you would choose life, so that you and your descendents might live! You can make this choice by loving the Lord your God, by obeying him, and committing yourself firmly to him. This is the key to your life. And if you love and obey the Lord, you will live long in the land the*

Lord swore to give your ancestors Abraham, Isaac, and Jacob (Deuteronomy 30:19-20, NLT).

If we love and obey God we are promised a long life and God's blessings—smells like success to me!

Noah's purpose was wrapped up in knowing God and obeying Him just as our purpose is hidden in Christ. All would perish but God would confirm His covenant in Noah—Noah was the new beginning. God's ultimate purpose was to preserve mankind and renew His covenant with man. Noah and building a ship was a practical outworking of their relationship and part of the means by which God would accomplish His end. The ship was a means to His end. It was walking in fellowship with God that kept Noah (and will keep us) blameless. Like Noah, when we fellowship in the light of Christ, our unfolding purpose is illuminated. After all, God gave step by step instructions—it was all outlined by the Lord...

So make yourself an ark of cypress wood; make rooms in it and coat it with pitch inside and out. This is how you are to build it: The ark is to be three hundred cubits long, fifty cubits wide and thirty cubits high. Make a roof for it, leaving below the roof an opening one cubit high all around. Put a door in the side of the ark and make lower, middle and upper decks. I am going to bring floodwaters on the earth to destroy all life under the heavens, every creature that has the breath of life in it. Everything on earth will perish. But I will establish my covenant with you, and you will enter the ark— you and your sons and your wife and your sons' wives with you. You are to bring into the ark two of all living creatures, male and female, to keep them alive with you. Two of every kind of bird, of every kind of animal and of every kind of creature that moves along the ground will come to you to be kept alive. You are to take every kind of food that is to be eaten and store it away as food for you and for them (Genesis 6:14-21).

The difference between success or failure for Noah was first and foremost obedience. When you step into the flow of what God is doing, when you take up His vision, when your purpose becomes God's purpose, what you are able to do can be extravagant—ever changing and ever growing. Everything behind you is divinely envisioned, supplied, planned, and appointed. Just stick close to the master and listen (i.e. obey). When you take up God's purpose and obey Him, nothing is impossible!

NOAH KNEW HIS 'WHY'— AND SO MUST WE!

Put yourself in Noah's shoes. Noah did what he was instructed to do because he knew his "why." How do I know? God told him exactly what to do and why he was doing it—and in each case, *Noah obeyed.*

Noah's "why" was outlined in Genesis 6:13-18. God declared that He would bring an "end of all flesh," and after the flood He would establish His covenant with Noah and his family. Noah's "why" involved more than saving his family, and a boatload of animals from destruction—God's covenant was at stake and failure was not an option!

Genesis 6:13-18 (NLT)

So God said to Noah, "I have decided to destroy all living creatures, for they have filled the earth with violence. Yes, I will wipe them all out along with the earth!

"Build a large boat from cypress wood and waterproof it with tar, inside and out. Then construct decks and stalls throughout its interior. Make the boat 450 feet long, 75 feet wide, and 45 feet high. Leave an 18-inch opening below the roof all the way around the boat. Put the door on the side, and build three decks inside the boat— lower, middle, and upper.

"Look! I am about to cover the earth with a flood that will destroy every living thing that breathes. Everything on earth will die. But I will confirm my covenant with you. So enter the boat—you and your wife and your sons and their wives."

Noah obeyed without hesitation. There was one word missing from Noah's vocabulary, and it's the word that stops many leaders from finding their purpose in life—*IMPOSSIBLE!*

Noah could have looked the situation over and said, "That's an impossible task." Or, he could have said, "This job is a recipe for failure; therefore, I won't even attempt to start." He didn't do or say anything remotely close to that. He rolled up his sleeves and got to work. The word impossible was not in his vocabulary! Because knowing God was knowing the Great Provider, the Great Creator, and His great faithfulness.

> *We are all faced with a series of great opportunities brilliantly disguised as impossible situations.*
> —CHARLES R. SWINDOLL[2]

I recently read the following story about the passion that can drive our purpose.

> There were two young boys, eight and nine years old, playing on a frozen pond. As they played, they skipped, jumped, and threw snowballs, and did all the things young boys do to have fun on a cold winter day. Suddenly the nine-year-old boy turned around to see his friend fall through a thin spot to the cold depths below. The piece of ice that broke came up and shut the hole like a trap door. On impulse, the nine-year-old ran over to a tree, grabbed a three-inch-thick branch, and ripped it off the tree. He ran to the spot where his friend had fallen through and began to beat the ice until he finally broke a hole eight feet wide. He found the hood of his friend's parka and pulled him up to safety.
>
> After the ambulance arrived and the paramedics checked the young boy's vital signs, it was announced that he was going to be fine, the crowd began to buzz. People started to wonder how such a young boy could break a three-inch-thick branch and ice that was equally thick? The crowd said, "Nine-year-olds can't break branches this thick, and ice that is too thick for a grown man to break." None of the answers they

came up with seemed to make sense. Then a hush came over the crowd, and an elderly gentleman came from the back of the crowd and said, "I can tell you why this young boy could break this branch and ice. He did it because there was no one here to tell him it was impossible."

This gentleman understood that the boy's purpose was so big, and the love for his friend was so great, that he did not bother to measure the branch to see if he would be able to break it. Love for his friend drove him over to that tree. Even if he wasn't strong enough to break the branch or the ice, he had to attempt to break it anyway. Why? Because the purpose driving him was overwhelming.[3]

In the same way this young boy could save his friend, the "love of Christ compels us" (2 Cor. 5:14-15) to accomplish our purpose in Him. That kind of love, though, is born out of relationship, fellowship. That is why Noah could persevere and build a ship and believe that the Father would keep His promise. His faith and perseverance was born out of fellowship-love for His Father.

3 MASTER KEYS TO UNLOCK YOUR 'WHY'

Without a proper understanding of "why" you were born, you will live without direction and purpose. Having no purpose in life is like a ship without a rudder or a car with no fuel. It was Mark Twain who said, *"The two most important days in life are the day you born and the day you discover the reason why."*[4]

We are called to know God.

Master Key #1. Talk—to the One who made you.

Doesn't it make more sense that if you want to discover WHY something was created you should go to the One who made it? In Genesis 6:13 God informed Noah of His plans… *"to put an end to all people, for the earth is filled with violence because of them. I am surely going to destroy both them and the earth."* How did Noah respond when God further informed him that he [Noah] was to build a massive boat *as a part of this grand plan?* From all indications, Noah didn't run home to complain to his wife about such a hard task. Nor did he ask his neighbors what they thought he ought to do. None of those things! What did he do? He kept talking to the ONE who was imparting purpose and direction—Noah was discovering his WHY!

The more Noah received from God, the more he understood his purpose. Makes sense to me—how about you?

A great place to start finding your purpose in God's plans is to spend time with the One who created you. Everyone was created with a purpose and you are no exception.

- Start by asking your heavenly Father to reveal to you why you are on planet Earth. The Psalmist declared, *"I praise you because I am fearfully and wonderfully made; your works are wonderful, I know that full well"* (Psalm 139:14).
- There is a big difference between "asking" and "demanding." It's never helpful in any relationship to make demands. Jesus said, *"Ask and it will be given to you; seek and you will find; knock and the door will be opened to you"* (Matthew 7:7).

- Don't be discouraged when you don't receive answers right away. Keep the dialogue going and remember what God said to Isaiah. *"For my thoughts are not your thoughts, neither are your ways my ways,' declares the Lord. 'As the heavens are higher than the earth, so are my ways higher than your ways and my thoughts than your thoughts'"* (Isaiah 55:8-9).

- Write it down. *"Then the Lord replied: 'Write down the revelation and make it plain on tablets so that a herald may run with it'"* (Habakkuk 2:2).

Master Key #2. Take time—to stop and listen.

So often what we call a conversation with God (prayer) is nothing more than reading out a laundry list of things we want. Sadly, we treat our prayer time as a job interview instead of building a love relationship with the One who created us. Prayer should be a dialogue, not a monologue!

When reading about Noah's relationship with God, it seems that Noah did more listening than talking. The Bible records Noah's standing before God. Genesis 6:8-9 says that *"But Noah found favor in the eyes of the Lord."* And, we are told that *"Noah was a righteous man, blameless among the people of his time, and he walked faithfully with God."* I would say that Noah is an excellent example of how we should conduct ourselves when we want to know about our "why."

For a dialogue to occur, it will require us to stop and listen to what the Lord is saying to us. It takes time to build a relationship with someone, and our relationship with the One who made us is just as important and more so.

> *Don't ask God to reveal His divine purpose for*
> *you by making demands. Rather, ask because*
> *in doing so, you are building a relationship*
> *with Him. That relationship is essential*
> *to understanding what He wants for you.*
> —DEBBIE CAUDLE[5]

How can we foster a closer relationship with the Father that is rightfully ours? In Mark and Patti Virkler's excellent book *How to Hear God's Voice,* they did a fantastic job highlighting the importance of developing a relationship with God.

Below is a sampling of the essential points:

- I can have a relationship with God through spiritual experiences rather than a dry monologue of simple mental prayer.
- The essence of prayer is my love relationship with the King of Kings, not simply going to Him to get things.
- The main purpose for learning to hear God's voice is so that I might really know Him—His heart, His joys, His desires, His hurts, His character, and His will.
- The Holy Spirit will mold my prayer life instead of me taking the principles of prayer God has shown me and reducing them to legalistic bondage.
- Christianity is much more than a code of ethics; it is much more than a religion. It is a direct

encounter with Him through the indwelling work of His Holy Spirit, which we freely receive as His gift to us.[6]

Master Key #3. Tune-up—before you crack up.

I think we can all agree that keeping our vehicles in proper working condition is a must. One of the most challenging aspects of parenting is when your teenagers begin to drive and you stress the importance of "watching the gauges" to make sure things are running smoothly. For some reason checking the oil levels are the bane of existence for most teenagers!

Staying tuned-up is not just about cars, trucks and farm equipment.

It applies to us humans as well.

As we get older, the maintaining and balancing of our lives becomes more of a challenge. I'm not necessarily referring to walking down steps or the everyday aches and pains that come with age. But the challenge often is about life's choices—and some of those choices are not between good and evil—but between what's good and what's best.

Maintaining a proper balance and a laser focus on where we are going is even a challenge for those of us who have a clear sense of purpose. Noah not only knew *what* he was doing but *why* he was attempting such a challenging job.

It's imperative to stay "tuned-up" because if we don't, no matter how much we think we know about God's plan and purpose for our lives, there will be a "crack-up" somewhere down the line!

One book stands above the rest on how to live a balanced life—it's the Bible (Basic Instructions Before Leaving Earth),

God's instruction book for every facet of our life, even how to live in balance.

> Psalm 16:11: *You make known to me the path of life; you will fill me with joy in your presence, with eternal pleasures at your right hand.*
>
> Proverbs 14:8: *The wisdom of the prudent is to give thought to their ways, but the folly of fools is deception.*

The best example of living a balanced life is found in the life of the most outstanding leader who ever lived—His name is Jesus.

Jesus then becomes a "pattern" on how to live a balanced life. Although we do not know much about his early life, we can gain much insight from one verse of Scripture—*And Jesus grew in wisdom and stature, and in favor with God and man.* (Luke 2:52). He was growing and maturing, and He became the model of putting life together in proper balance.

The Scripture gives us a snapshot of four characteristics of Jesus' growth. I would say that these four areas are essential for us as well.

1. Mentally—Jesus grew in wisdom. *"If any of you lacks wisdom, you should ask God, who gives generously to all without finding fault, and it will be given to you"* (James 1:5).

2. Physically—Jesus grew in wisdom and stature. *"You're bought with a price therefore you're not your own... therefore glorify God in your body."* (1 Corinthians 6:19-20).

3. Spiritually—Jesus grew in wisdom and in stature and in favor with God. *"Grow in grace and knowledge of your Lord Jesus Christ"* (2 Peter 3:18).

4. Socially—Jesus grew in wisdom and in stature and in favor with God and man. *"Live in harmony with one another"* (Romans 12:16).

Living in balance means an understanding that when we discover our "why," we will strive to maintain a good relationship between body, soul, and spirit.

ONE MORE THOUGHT...

As I said earlier, Jesus was the world's greatest leader. Jesus became the world's most outstanding leader, not because He commanded a large army or amassed a large fortune to fund His ministry. He was successful in His mission on earth because He knew His WHY—Mark 10:45 says, *"For even the Son of Man did not come to be served, but to serve, and to give his life as a ransom for many."*

Without a shadow of a doubt, Jesus knew He was in this world at the discretion and direction of His Father as a sacrifice for our sins. He was crystal clear as to why He was here and who sent Him. His WHY—reason for being here, enabled His WHAT—what He had to do (purpose). This clarity of reason and purpose is seen in His confident statements in scripture:

John 9:4: *"As long as it is day, we must do the works of him who sent me. Night is coming, when no one can work."*

John 10:10: *"The thief comes only to steal and kill and destroy; I have come that they may have life, and have it to the full."*

John 13:13: *"You call me 'Teacher' and 'Lord,' and rightly so, for that is what I am."*

John 16:28: *"I came from the Father and entered the world; now I am leaving the world and going back to the Father."*

You and I have been created for our own unique WHY. We can no longer wander through any aspect of life. We MUST be purposeful about everything we do—the enemy of your soul loves passivity because he knows it's a pathway to failure.

Life is never made unbearable by circumstances,
but only by lack of meaning and purpose.
—**Viktor Frankl**[7]

ENDNOTES

1. https://www.success.com/17-inspiring-quotes-to-help-you-live-a-life-of-purpose/ accessed November 7, 2020.

2. https://impossiblehq.com/33-more-impossible-quotes/ accessed November 14, 2020.

3. Larry DiAngi, *How to be Purpose Driven*, (Erie, PA: Larry DiAngi Productions, 1998) 14-15.

4 https://thestrive.co/find-your-purpose-quotes/ accessed November 8, 2020.

5. https://www.bydivinedesignforwomen.com/meet-debbie accessed November 8, 2020.

6   Mark and Patti Virkler, *How to Hear God's Voice,* (Shippensburg, PA: Destiny Image Publishers, 2005) 22-23.

7. https://thestrive.co/find-your-purpose-quotes/ accessed November 8, 2020.

3

WE ARE ALL IN THE SAME BOAT

(It's a Real Zoo in Here)

We must learn to live together as brothers or perish together as fools.
—MARTIN LUTHER KING[1]

Resist him, standing firm in the faith, because you know that the family of believers throughout the world is undergoing the same kind of sufferings.
—1 PETER 5:9

Can you imagine Noah's surprise?

While he is busy cutting lumber, and preparing other necessary supplies to construct the world's largest boat, suddenly animals of every shape, size, and type begin to show up at his construction site!

What a shock—but it shouldn't have caught him off guard. After all, the Lord had already given him instructions, and they were precise. Genesis 6:19-21:

> *You are to bring into the ark two of all living creatures, male and female, to keep them alive with you. Two of every kind of bird, of every kind of animal and of every kind of creature that moves along the ground will come to you to be kept alive. You are to take every kind of food that is to be eaten and store it away as food for you and for them.*

Noah is about to discover the meaning of a trite, old saying, "We are all in the same boat..." and take it to another level. I don't know about you, but the thought of trying to corral so many different types of creatures and then be responsible for feeding, cleaning, and picking up after them (you know what I'm talking about) is more than the mind can comprehend. But, Noah and his team (family) did whatever was necessary to make sure all who were in their care arrived at their destination safely.

What does the phrase *"We are all in the same boat"* actually mean? The most widely accepted explanation says:

> There are quite a few speculations about where the term "all in the same boat" originated. One of the most popular comes from the sinking of the Titanic when people from all classes were in the same situation after the ship struck the iceberg.[2]

How does the *"We are all in the same boat"* idea translate to us today? The phrase can mean different things to different people. But, to me, it more than implies the attitude of teamwork.

I DON'T THINK FOR A MINUTE NOAH DID ALL THE WORK HIMSELF—HE HAD TO DEVELOP A TEAM AROUND HIM TO ACCOMPLISH SUCH A GREAT TASK—AND SO MUST WE!

Noah understood the importance of teamwork. *Ark Building 101* was the product of Noah and his family working together toward a common goal. And, what was the goal? In this case, it ensured that all the instructions were followed, and everyone was doing their job. There was a planet to save, and without teamwork, the ark would have sunk before it ever floated ten feet!

> *I can accept failure. Everyone fails at something. But I can't accept not trying [no hard work]. Talent wins games, but teamwork and intelligence win championships.*
> —**MICHAEL JORDAN**[3]

4 DEFINING TRAITS ABOUT ARK BUILDING '101' THAT YOU NEED TO KNOW

(HINT—IT'S ALL ABOUT TEAMWORK)

1. Teamwork is a model to ensure equal opportunity— but can never guarantee equal outcome.

Sharing similar experiences (on a team) doesn't mean the outcomes will be the same for everyone. As Linda Graham said, "I heard that we are all in the same boat, but it's not like that. We are in the same storm, but not in the same boat. Your ship could be shipwrecked and mine might not be. Or vice versa.[4]

The fact is everyone has a choice—you can work to develop a team attitude, or you can risk it all and travel alone. You can build your boat and row just as hard and as fast as you can—that's always an option. But understand one thing—you will only go as far as your talents and abilities will take you. I'm not against individual entrepreneurship—oh, no. But every successful entrepreneur will tell you that whatever success they enjoyed was because they learned the secret of teamwork. If your dreams are to be accomplished, it will take more than individual talent to get you there.

Andrew Carnegie was one of the world's most successful entrepreneurs (in the history of business). He didn't just start a company that happened to make steel; he revolutionized an entire industry. Carnegie famously said: "Teamwork is the ability to work together toward a common vision, the ability to direct individual accomplishments toward organizational objectives. It {teamwork} is the fuel that allows common people to attain uncommon results."

> [He was] one of the pioneers of the Industrial Revolution. Some entrepreneurs are famous for starting businesses, Andrew Carnegie helped launch an entire industry (the steel industry). He couldn't have done that on his own. He needed a team to help him. In the quotation, he talks about how teams united in purpose can achieve uncommon results. Considering that he sold his steel company to J.P. Morgan for about $370 billion in today's dollars (as a proportion of GDP), it's safe to say he practiced what he preached.[5]

Some may think that working as a team will limit opportunities or stifle growth. What do you think would have happened to Noah had he taken the Lone Ranger approach?

I cannot imagine Noah telling his family to take a vacation while attempting to do all the work himself. I can almost guarantee you that Noah saw the challenge before him and knew it would take teamwork to make the impossible possible!

Instead of going it alone, consider what happens when you work as a team. Working as a team...

- magnifies your talents and abilities.
- opens you up to new ideas and stimulates creativity.
- allows your value to be multiplied exponentially.
- places you in an arena to see the success of a team working together.
- combines your strengths with other team members to create a dynamo of productivity.
- will give you a greater sense of pride and ownership in what the team is trying to accomplish.
- shares the responsibility of risk-taking.
- fosters individual growth and thereby benefits the team.

2. *Teamwork Makes You Happier.*

Recently, The Happiness Index, a tool that helps organizations measure the key employee engagement and satisfaction, created a "Happiness Formula" that states the organization's success is in direct correlation to the happiness of each team member. They found that there is a link between how people feel and how that feeling affects their performance. Their research highlighted the top five most critical components of working as a team, feeling happy, and increasing production.

- Feeling valued—This is the most important factor for employees and employers. In our view, the essence of good teamwork is that every individual feels valued. This enables people to perform at their best.

- Trusting the people you work with—People who are trusted by their peers are more likely to work together, share ideas and feel comfortable enough to think creatively.

- Quality of leadership—All teams need leaders. Effective teamwork is facilitated by leaders, although these people are not necessarily the most senior people in a group.

- Ability to speak your mind openly and honestly— Teamwork is a group agreement on how people engage with each other. To be at its best, an open and respectful dialogue is essential.

- Having control over your work—Autonomy can be difficult when job roles are functional. Yet people demand the ability to go about their job in a way that works for them, bring their own ideas and improve how things are done.[6]

Most leadership experts agree that one key element in developing a happy, productive team starts at the top. Research on the question of a happy team was conducted at the University of

Warwick in England. The study points out that *"happy employees are up to 20 percent more productive than unhappy employees. And who couldn't benefit from a happiness boost?"*[7]

It is incumbent on the leader of the team to ensure there is an atmosphere of success. A key element in the happiness equation is learning to manage expectations. Even though Noah received his instructions directly from the Lord, I am sure he informed his family (team) what the expectations were. Keeping your team "in the dark" will only increase apprehension and lead to a negative atmosphere.

Here are three ways to improve and manage the expectations of the team.

1) Learn the difference between managed and unrealistic expectations.

One of the challenges that strong leaders face is the "Let's get the job done today" attitude. Disappointments usually follow unrealistic expectations. A good way to manage expectations is to learn to appreciate and understand how others think and work. Sitting at the head of the table and looking around the room is not a good way to decide if your teammates' ideas are worth considering. Once you understand a little more about the team, you will be more likely to consider their ideas and balance your expectations with their abilities.

2) Learn to compromise.

Here's a thought—you don't have to be right all the time! Learn to keep the "main thing" the main thing. When you view "winning all the time" as a battle, you will eventually wear yourself out. Learn to save yourself for what really matters! Be prepared to concede to the possible benefits of a suggestion and the time necessary to give it consideration.

3) Practice servanthood.

If you want to endure less conflict, learn to serve rather than be served. In difficult situations, you can always find something to agree upon and give it your best effort to maintain peace and order.

3. *Teamwork Maximizes Effectiveness.*

You can use your imagination and picture Noah assigning each family member (his team) certain areas of responsibility. Ark building was not going to become a "one-man show", but rather a team working together for the entire project's success. Noah instinctively knew that in order for him to obey the instructions, one person was NOT going to make it happen. I am convinced that ONE person rarely achieves what a dedicated team can accomplish.

> *The way a team plays as a whole determines its success. You may have the greatest bunch of individual stars in the world, but if they don't play together, the club won't be worth a dime.*
>
> —BABE RUTH[8]

A wise team leader will understand that each individual is uniquely gifted to add value to the team's overall success. Therefore, it is incumbent on leadership to find and select the "right" person for the job.

Below are five types of individuals you need to consider when building your team:

Five Types of Individuals You Must Have on Your Team

1) The Vision Caster

As the team leader, you are most likely the visionary. You can see the project as a whole from start to finish. Casting a vision with measurable goals will infuse the team with confidence as they move forward. It's hard to lead a team if you don't know where you are going!

2) The Strategist

Although the visionary is also considered a strategist, it is vital to have a person who is not shy when it comes to the "nuts and bolts" of the project. The visionary and the strategist will work hand in glove to oversee the project from start to finish.

3) The Communicator

This member of the team is someone who does more than talk. They have a unique ability to communicate the goals and strategies of the team. This person connects all members of the team by facilitating the transfer of ideas and messages.

4) The Analyst

Every team must have this person. Why? The analyst looks for and tries to solve problems before they sink the entire project. These folks are the problem solvers; without them, most teams would fall into the dark hole of confusion.

5) The Worker

This team member is willing to go the extra mile to get the job done. He or she is not afraid to roll up his sleeves and lead the way to the project's challenging parts. These folks are self-starters and will need little or no motivation to see it through. Of course, the best plan of action is to have everyone on the team infected with the energy of the worker bee![9]

4. Teamwork Builds Commitment to a Shared Goal.

Commitment to take action is an essential characteristic of an effective team. When trust is built, team members can agree to move forward and take action based on the group's collective wisdom. Remember, just talking about something does not ensure success. An ordinary team becomes an "Extraordinary Team" when it executes the plan!

> *There's a difference between interest and commitment. When you're interested in doing something, you do it only when circumstances permit. When you're committed to something, you accept no excuses, only results.*
> —KEN BLANCHARD[10]

Commitment to take action is just the first step. After commitments are made, a smart leader will begin building and keeping commitments among the team members.

Firstly, Build the Commitment by:

- Getting everyone involved. Allowing everyone's input sounds easy, but I can tell you that it can be challenging from personal experience. NO team will ever agree one-hundred percent of the time. It's up to the leader to make sure that areas of disagreement are heard and worked out so the team can move forward as one unit.

- Deciding to move forward. A "no decision" is the worst possible outcome. Procrastination is a sure way to kill the dream!

- Establishing a deadline. Establishing benchmarks for completing a specific task is one way of making sure that team members are committed.

- Starting with small steps. It's the age-old principle that says if you're going on a journey of a thousand miles, you must take the first small step. In other words, learn to take small steps before attempting to take on much larger projects.

Secondly, Keeping the Commitment.

- Being on the same page does not mean everyone will agree with every new idea or a contrary opinion. If there is common respect among each team member, you can be assured that half the battle is already won. You can always have the freedom to disagree, but strive never to become disagreeable!

- There is a phrase in the Bible that talks about being in "one accord." It doesn't mean that everyone will agree to walk in lock-step, but it does mean that each team member is committed to loving God with all their heart, soul, mind, and strength and loving one another even when disagreements arise.

- The meaning of *one accord* comes from two words: "homo," meaning "the same," and "thumos," which means "passion." We are to work toward a common goal with the same zeal and passion for completing the assignment with joy and excellence.

The great apostle Paul said it best in Philippians 2:2 (NLT), *"Then make me truly happy by agreeing wholeheartedly with each other, loving one another, and working together with one mind and purpose."*

ONE MORE THOUGHT…

We must always remember that Jesus Christ was the ultimate team leader. We will learn the importance of building a successful team as we consider how Jesus motivated a small group of men to change the world. Although we can learn from many successful leaders, a close examination of Jesus, the ultimate leader, reveals a roadmap to success. DON'T PRE-JUDGE

I challenge you to spend time in the Word (specifically the Gospels) and discover how Jesus chose some of the most unlikely people in the world to take on the biggest challenge of their lives. You may also be amazed that Jesus did not search out the *crème da la crème* of the religious establishment, nor the upper crust of society to form His team.

Nancy Ortberg observed that Jesus never underestimated anyone when it came to selecting those who would become a part of His team.

> Perhaps Jesus, understanding that everyone would expect him to develop his team out of the cream of the crop, was trying to help us understand that his gospel transforms everyone.

While no one would suggest that you ignore talent and competency and character, the Bible is full of ordinary people doing extraordinary things because of what God did through them. The common denominator is not their abilities; it's their relationship with God. Acts 4:13 goes on to say, "People were astonished because these were unschooled, ordinary men who had been with Jesus." We are blinded and misled by the outer trappings of success: resumes, bank accounts, job titles, and physical appearance. But those are not the filters Jesus used to choose.[11]

It's important to remember that if you find yourself about to embark on building a boat that will become the largest floating zoo known to man, choose your team wisely, train them, and—most of all—lead them to dry land!

After all, we're all in the same boat!

ENDNOTES

1. Martin Luther King quote from March 22, 1964, speech in St. Louis. https://www.latimes.com/archives/la-xpm-1998-jan-19-me-10002 -story.html accessed February 10, 2021.

2. https://www.gingersoftware.com/content/phrases/all-in-the-same -boat accessed February 10, 2021.

3. *I Can't Accept Not Trying: Michael Jordan on the Pursuit of Excellence.* (San Francisco, CA: Harper, 1994). p. 129 https://en.wikiquote.org/ wiki/Michael_Jordan accessed February 10, 2020.

4. https://lindagraham-mft.net/we-are-not-in-the-same-boat/ accessed February 10, 2021.

5. https://www.entrepreneur.com/article/269941 accessed February 11, 2021.

6. https://thehappinessindex.com/happiness/how-happiness-creates -success/ accessed February 11, 2021.

7. https://www.atlassian.com/blog/teamwork/the-importance-of -teamwork accessed February 11, 2021.

8. https://www.tameday.com/teamwork-quotes/ accessed February 13, 2021.

9. "5 Types of People You Want on Your Team," https:// leadinglikeachampion.com/ 5-types-of-people-you-want-on-your -team/ accessed February 18, 2022.

10. https://www.passiton.com/inspirational-quotes/7320-theres-a -difference-between-interest-accessed February 13, 2021.

11. https://www.christianitytoday.com/pastors/2016/september-web -exclusives/odd-teamwork-of-jesus.html February 14, 2021.

4

How Big Do You Build?

(Build Big Enough to Accommodate Your Growing Dream)

GET ALL MY DUCKS IN A ROW

Do not wait; the time will never be just right. Start where you stand, and work with whatever tools you may have at your command, and better tools will be found as you go along.

—George Herbert[1]

So make yourself an ark of cypress wood; make rooms in it and coat it with pitch inside and out. This is how you are to build it: The ark is to be three hundred cubits long, fifty cubits wide and thirty cubits high. Make a roof for it, leaving below the roof an opening one cubit high all around. Put a door in the side of the ark and make lower, middle and upper decks.

—Genesis 6:14-16

The Lord was never one to waste words.

"Noah, I want you to build an ark, and here are the blueprints. So, get cracking, no time to waste."

The instructions were clear. No ambiguity. No explanation is needed. Of all living creatures on the Earth, the Lord found Noah to be the only one blameless enough to be entrusted with such a monumental task. If the job was going to get done, it was up to Noah.

> *Noah was a righteous man, the only blameless person living on earth at the time, and he walked in close fellowship with God. Noah was the father of three sons: Shem, Ham, and Japheth* (Genesis 6:9-10 NLT).

You might say Noah became the world's first superhero!

Noah would build something the world had never seen, to prepare for something the world had never experienced. Following the instructions was crucial. This project was not going to be some new type of boat, or sailing vessel—it was to be an Ark—a big floating box.

Pastor John MacArthur observed:

> Now you need to understand the word "ark." It's the word tebah in Hebrew. It means a box. Make a big box. Noah knew what a boat was about—boats have always been built similarly. They have sloped sides and a curved bottom. That's not what God told him to build. He said build a box; just a big, rectangular, wooden box. A chest might be another way to view it. Not shaped like a boat, not shaped like a ship, wasn't designed to sail, and it wasn't designed to be propelled.

It didn't need to have a thin bow to cut through the water when it was being propelled by oars, as they were in ancient times, or propelled by the wind in the sail because it wasn't going to be propelled. It was a cruise to nowhere. There wasn't anywhere to go. It was only designed to float. There were no oars, there were no sails, there was no pilot, there was no captain, there was no steering wheel, there was no rudder, there was no navigator. It was just a box.[2]

While it's true the Ark wasn't designed to be the world's fastest or the mightiest ship that ever sailed the seven seas, this floating box still had to be big enough to accommodate the vision God imparted to Noah. What would have happened had Noah said to his family, *"The Lord's instructions were merely suggestions on how big we are to build. I feel certain He will bless whatever we do."* Do you think that kind of attitude would be acceptable to the Lord?

The New Living Translation gives us details in plain English, so you don't have to grab your computer and google the calculation of cubits' length and other Old Testament measurements.

Build a large boat from cypress wood and waterproof it with tar, inside and out. Then construct decks and stalls throughout its interior. Make the boat 450 feet long, 75 feet wide, and 45 feet high. Leave an 18-inch opening below the roof all the way around the boat. Put the door on the side, and build three decks inside the boat—lower, middle, and upper. "Look! I am about to cover the earth with a flood that will destroy every living thing that breathes. Everything on earth will die. But I will confirm my covenant with you. So enter the boat—you and your wife and your sons and their wives. Bring a pair of every kind of animal—a male and a female—into the boat with you to keep them alive during the flood. Pairs of every kind of bird, and every kind of animal, and every kind of small animal that scurries along the ground, will come to you to be kept alive. And be sure to take on board enough food for your family and for all the animals."

So Noah did everything exactly as God had commanded him. (Genesis 6:14-22 NLT).

The Ark was going to take approximately one hundred years to construct, and when completed, it was going to be roughly the size of a modern football stadium.

To give you some idea of how big this floating box was going to be, Henry Morris stated the following in his book, *The Genesis Record*:

> The total volumetric capacity of the Ark was approximately 1,400,000 cubic feet, which is equal to the volumetric capacity of 522 standard livestock cars such as used on modern American railroads. Since it is known that about 240 sheep can be transported in one stock car, a total of over 125,000 sheep could have been carried on the Ark. The ark would have had to have been turned completely vertical before it could be tipped over, it was so stable. It's relative length, six times greater than its width, would tend to keep it from being subjected to wave forces because wave forces aren't that long. And even if it got sideways,

there was no single wave force that would hit the total ship. Furthermore, it would tend, rather than going through the waves, to ride with the waves and because of the sheer weight of it, with all of its occupants, it would be virtually impossible to turn it over.[3]

Remember Noah did all of this without the benefit of Lowe's, 84 Lumber, or Home Depot to order his supplies!

You may be wondering how the Ark has anything to do with what is going on in your life. Are there any lessons we can learn about building your dream from Noah's approach to building the Ark?

Yes, absolutely.

Consider a critical statement about Noah in Hebrews 11:7 (NLT).

> *It was by faith that Noah built a large boat to save his family from the flood. He obeyed God, who warned him about things that had never happened before. By his faith Noah condemned the rest of the world, and he received the righteousness that comes by faith.*

Did you catch it? Noah's motivation was based on faith, and his faith was put into action when he hammered the first peg into the wood. Noah was obedient to God's release of the vision about coming events even though there wasn't any Biblical record of anything like a flood before this time. Genesis 2:5-6 tells us,

> *Now no shrub had yet appeared on the earth and no plant had yet sprung up, for the Lord God had not sent rain on the earth and there was no one to work*

the ground, but streams came up from the earth and watered the whole surface of the ground.

A Divine irrigation system watered the Earth, and the idea of rain or a flood would have been a foreign language to Noah.

Here's my point—*for faith to be genuine, it must be put into action!* For over one hundred years, Noah did not let go of the promise he received from God. The vision was so strong that nothing or no one could stop him from completing the task. That's the kind of commitment to a dream that will carry you through no matter what "floods" come your way.

> *Twenty years from now, you will be more disappointed by the things you didn't do than by the ones you did. So, throw off the bowlines. Sail away from the safe harbor. Catch the trade winds in your sails. Explore. Dream. Discover.*
>
> —MARK TWAIN.[4]

If you are going to build your dream (whatever that looks like to you), make sure you build big enough. Why? SIZE DOES MATTER WHEN IT COMES TO YOUR DREAM.

- Don't limit the size of your dream based on what you see around you.

- Don't limit the size of your dream based on what you feel inside of you.

- Don't limit the size of your dream based on what others say about you.

■ Don't limit the size of your dream based on the idea that "it's never been done before."

The only roadblock to your dream is the person staring back at you in the mirror!

Take it from Noah; nothing short of proper preparation and building according to the instructions would have sufficed. As Chris Widener famously said, *"Vision is the spectacular that inspires us to carry out the mundane."*[5]

3 KEY STEPS TO TAKE WHEN BUILDING YOUR ARK (DREAM)

1. *Stop Arguing with Yourself.*

How do you "argue" with yourself? Simple. By constantly engaging in negative self-talk. It's the most common everyday conversation that most of us have. Jack Canfield said, *"Researchers estimate that we think about 50,000 to 70,000 thoughts a day— and that about 80% of those thoughts are negative. That is a crazy amount of negative self-talk!"*[6]

It's essential to understand the devastating effects it can have on your dream. Life coach Elizabeth Scott offered the following definition of negative self-talk:

> Basically, negative self-talk is any inner dialogue you have with yourself that may be limiting your ability to believe in yourself and your own abilities, and to reach your potential. It is any thought that diminishes your ability to make positive changes in your life or your confidence in yourself to do so. So, negative self-talk

can not only be stressful, but it can really stunt your success.[7]

Negative self-talk will:

- Steal your joy by keeping you focused on the negatives.
- Give you a false sense of "I am always right, and they are always wrong."
- Divert your attention from future possibilities by always taking you back to past hurt and disappointment.
- Will keep you trapped in a never-ending cycle of fear, resentment, and stress.
- Always keep you thinking the worst is going to happen (and it never does).
- Weaken your immune system, as well as change your hormone levels to induce more stress.

One of the best ways to reduce or even stop negative self-talk is to recognize when it happens and substitute it with a positive self-talk attitude. Replacing the negative with the positive is not a pie-in-the-sky approach to living. The apostle Paul gave us a roadmap to handle the negatives when he said,

> *Finally, brothers and sisters, whatever is true, whatever is noble, whatever is right, whatever is pure, whatever is lovely, whatever is admirable—if anything is excellent or praiseworthy—think about such things* (Philippians 4:8).

REMEMBER: What you constantly think about (and discuss in your mind) you will eventually become. You can change your behavior by right thinking and positive self-talk.

2. Watch Your Daily Routine.

Noah faced a seemingly impossible task. No one had to tell him that this job would take an extraordinary effort and a massive amount of time to complete. He became a wise master builder because he focused on what was in front of him. There isn't any doubt that he also scheduled his daily routine to avoid waking up each day without any idea of what he was doing. To my way of thinking, Noah was successful because he decided not to "wing-it" but to "plan-it" to completion!

> *When people don't have a routine or structure to their day it can cause increased stress and anxiety, as well as overwhelming feelings, lack of concentration, and focus.*
> —RACHEL GOLDMAN, PhD.[8]

Do you understand that many people (including those in leadership positions) have NO consistent daily routine? It's hard to believe that anyone can be successful without an established daily routine. But, the fact remains that many people have no idea what a daily schedule will do for them. It seems for some, a *"Que Sera, Sera"* or "Whatever will be will be" approach is the best way to live. I have a feeling Noah would tell you that is a nutty way to build an Ark!

It's important to note that while a daily routine is a good thing, I am not suggesting that the "one size fits all" approach is proper. Each one of us will have to determine a daily routine that works best.

But, there are a few positive outcomes embedded in a daily routine that apply to everyone.

A daily routine will:

- Increase your productivity.
- Decrease your level of stress.
- Over time, it will form positive habits and eliminate negative habits.
- Focus on what's important (priorities) over what is necessary.
- Create a daily roadmap to complete even the most challenging assignments.
- Cut down on the frivolous time wasters and make better use of our day.
- Eliminate the "I will do it tomorrow" syndrome.

3. Don't Listen to the Monday Morning Quarterbacks.

According to Dictionary.com, a Monday morning quarterback is a person who criticizes the actions or decisions of others after the fact, using hindsight to assess situations and specify alternative solutions.[9] In other words, this is a person who loves to sit back and criticize those who are engaging in the daily battle to pursue their dreams and goals.

Can you imagine how many critics Noah had? The Bible does not give us many specifics, but as a human nature student, I can say with a modicum of certainty that this "preacher of righteousness" (see 2 Peter 2:5) had his share of people who wanted to tell him how crazy he was.

There will always be those who would rather criticize you for what you're doing instead of getting in the game themselves. If we are not careful, we will be more concerned about what the nay-sayers say than fulfilling our purpose on planet earth.

The greatest leader who ever lived, the Lord Jesus Christ, faced more than His share of critics. You might say the Monday Morning Quarterbacks (made up of the religious crowd) were always front and center, ready to admonish Him for what they thought He was doing wrong.

- In Matthew 11:19, He was called a glutton and a drunk.
- In Matthew 9:11, He was accused of hanging out with the wrong people.
- In John 8:48, they accused Him of having a demon.
- In Mark 3:21, they said He was out of His mind!

Jesus set the example when dealing with critics. Instead of lashing out and defending Himself, the apostle Peter gave us insight into how He handled it:

> *He committed no sin, and no deceit was found in his mouth. When they hurled their insults at him, he did not retaliate; when he suffered, he made no threats. Instead, he entrusted himself to him who judges justly. He himself bore our sins in his body on the cross, so that we might die to sins and live for righteousness; by his wounds you have been healed* (1 Peter 2:22-24).

Here's my point:

Had Jesus spent all of His time defending Himself and allowing the Monday Morning Quarterbacks to discourage Him from His mission, He would have never gone to the cross to die for our sins.

Apparently, Jesus never felt He had to stop and lay out a defense to His critics. And, neither should we. I find many times when Jesus faced off with His critics, He just stayed silent. And, for that, they hated Him even more. When He did give them an answer, it was not what they were expecting and was usually framed in a question—which put them on the spot (see John 8:1-11).

When you're faced with the Monday Morning Quarterbacks, be like Jesus!

ONE MORE THOUGHT...

I don't think anyone would dispute the fact that Noah was faced with a difficult task. His desire to obey God was greater than the obstacles before him. In those hundred-plus years of building, I am sure he endured times when he wanted to quit. But, despite adversity, setbacks, and detours, he persevered to overcome them.

What can we learn from Noah's attitude?

- Noah was obedient to the instructions. He followed a plan.
- Noah wasn't heard speaking until after the flood. He didn't complain.
- Noah refused to give up or give in. He overcame by faith in God's Word.
- Noah was not fazed by his critics. He refused to be swayed by negativity.

- Noah was unafraid of hard work. He knew lazy people would never build the Ark.

- Noah didn't work alone. He knew the importance of teamwork to get the job done.

To realize our dream, we must take to heart what George Whitefield said, "Press forward. Do not stop, do not linger in your journey, but strive for the mark set before you."[10]

ENDNOTES

1. https://www.success.com/17-motivational-quotes-to-help-you -achieve-your-dreams/ accessed March 1, 2021.

2. https://www.gty.org/library/sermons-library/90-257/noahs-ark-of -faith accessed March 1, 2021.

3. Henry Morris, *The Genesis Record,* (San Diego, CA: Creation—Life Publishers, 1976), 181.

4. https://www.rd.com/list/dream-big-quotes/ accessed March 2, 2021.

5. https://www.success.com/7-steps-to-achieve-your-dream/ accessed March 2, 2021.

6. Jack Canfield, "5 Tips to Stop Negative Self-Talk Once & For All," https://www.jackcanfield.com/blog/negative-self-talk/ accessed March 3, 2021.

7. Elizabeth Scott, MS. "The Toxic Effects of Negative Self-Talk," https://www.verywellmind.com/negative-self-talk-and-how-it-affects -us-4161304 accessed March 3, 2021.

8. Rachel Goldman, PHD., https://www.verywellmind.com/the -importance-of-keeping-a-routine-during-stressful-times-4802638/ accessed March 20, 2021.

9. https://www.dictionary.com/browse/monday-morning-quarterback/ accessed March 20, 2021.

10. https://www.success.com/17-motivational-quotes-to-help-you
-achieve-your-dreams/ March 27, 2021.

5

DREAMS ARE NOT BUILT OVERNIGHT

(One of the Only Things That's an Overnight Success Is a Sunrise)

Somehow over the years, people have gotten the impression that Wal-Mart was...just this great idea that turned into an overnight success. But...it was an outgrowth of everything we'd been doing since [1945]... And like most overnight successes, it was about twenty years in the making.

—SAM WALTON[1]

In the six hundredth year of Noah's life, on the seventeenth day of the second month—on that day all the springs of the great deep burst forth, and the floodgates of the heavens were opened. And rain fell on the earth forty days and forty nights.

—GENESIS 7:11-12

The seemingly impossible task was complete. It was now time to gather up the family, the animals, and prepare for the impending flood. You might say that Noah was the first in a long line of leaders who took years, in his case approximately 100, to become an overnight success!

Think about the fact that Noah did the job without formal training in boat building, a financial base or a network of entrepreneurs to assist him. Noah didn't have the internet with its countless websites to teach him how to be successful. Despite his limitations, he was determined to finish the task he was assigned to do.

In our day, we have many books, articles, etc., on leadership. These "experts" offer advice, strategy, and resources to become successful wherever your passion takes you. However, very few emphasize the importance of viewing *success as a journey to take and not a final destination to make.* Far too many emphasize the trappings of success without a proper understanding of what it takes to arrive at the so-called "success destination."

The definition of success indeed varies from person to person. But, I find it interesting that a common belief among many is expressed in the brief sampling below:

- For me, success was always going to be a Lamborghini. But now I've got it; it just sits on my drive. —CURTIS JACKSON [50 Cent][2]

- Achieving success is an unquantifiable notion—indeed, success carries with it an aura of money and power, and things like that, which—certainly for me—would be detrimental. —SIR CAMERON MACKINTOSH[3]

- Success is whatever humiliation everyone has agreed to compete for. —JAMES RICHARDSON[4]

What does success look like to you?

Is it just about money, power, or the accumulation of things? Could there possibly be more to success than what you have been told in the past?

TWO CRUCIAL questions that need to be asked if you want to get to the heart of individual success:

Question #1. Do you know why you are here (on planet earth)?

All your skills and abilities were created on purpose for God's purposes. There are no accidents or mistakes with God. You don't have to have an engineering degree to understand that every manufactured product was designed with its purpose (use) in mind. I doubt the inventor of the microwave rolled out his finished product and said, "I don't know what this thing will do, maybe you can use it to wash your dishes!" Likewise, God never made anything without its purpose in mind, and He never created anything just for fun. And, when He made you, He didn't make a mistake.

The Bible is filled with God's intentional nature:

- He purposed to save Noah and his family (and the animals) even before the Ark's construction (Genesis 6-9).
- He purposed to have Solomon build the Temple long before Solomon was born (2 Samuel 7).

- He purposed that the virgin Mary would have a child who would be the savior of the world before the Holy Spirit came to her (Isaiah 7:14).

- He purposed that Paul would take the Gospel to the Gentiles before he sent Ananias to pray for him (Acts 9:15).

An individual who lives without a purpose is like a fish out of water. Fish were not created to live on dry land. It is a foreign environment that will lead to death. There are millions of people walking around like a fish out of water. They know they are still alive and just barely breathing—they just don't know why they are still here!

> *Trusting God completely means having faith that He knows what is best for your life. You expect Him to keep His promises, help you with problems, and do the impossible when necessary.*
> —RICK WARREN[5]

Question #2. Are you willing to pay the price to reach your potential?

A definition of potential states that it (potential) *is existing in possibility: capable of development into actuality.*[6] Simply put, *potential* means abilities that are latent but possible.

The *existing in possibility* part of the definition of potential is seen every year when the major sports (NFL, NBA, MLB, NHL) leagues hold a draft. In the draft, players are selected, not on what they have accomplished as professional athletes but on their potential. Each team must decide, *based solely on the player's past performance*, if there is enough potential to justify paying out millions of dollars in contracts. Mind you, no baskets have been sunk yet, and no home runs have been hit yet, and it's the YET that the owners are paying for. The real world doesn't usually work that way. In most organizations spending millions of dollars based on what someone *might do* doesn't usually happen.

Those who have reached a certain level of success will tell you that it takes time, hard work, and a bucket full of sweat to grow to become an overnight success. You cannot always act in a manner that is inconsistent with the way you see yourself. It is sad to know that most people on planet Earth will never discover what they can do, while others settle for only a portion of their true potential. We all indeed have the same opportunity to fully use the gifts, talents, abilities, and capabilities that have been put within us. The question is, will we exercise the option to maximize our potential?

I have discovered that each step along the road to finding my potential was a price to pay. Now, when I speak about paying the price, many people will simply turn and run the other way. They don't want to hear that there may be things that need to be redefined or tossed out altogether. Let's be honest, most of us DON'T want to hear about giving up anything. It's much easier to say it's just not worth giving up things that might hinder our growth. I understand that—but if you want to succeed in life, you have to know that ALL success comes with a price—NO EXCEPTIONS!

The first step in "counting the cost" of success is learning the value of taking personal responsibility. Leadership coach Fredy Romero made a profound observation about the importance of taking personal responsibility and how it relates to the cost of success:

> When you blame circumstances, you are conditioning yourself to be a helpless victim. When you take responsibility for your current state, you can now take control of what you'll do next.
>
> You and only you can accept responsibility. My wife isn't responsible for my actions. Neither are my friends. What I do solely depends on me, my beliefs, my thinking. I am ultimately responsible for how I respond when I get into trouble and how I get out of that trouble.
>
> You want to be great? Take responsibility.
>
> If I want to grow my business by 100% this year, I need to take the time and put in the work to grow it that much. I need to invest in myself and this business to hit that goal. I cannot blame anyone for not achieving what I set out to do. At the end of the year, only the man in the mirror is responsible for the results I get.
>
> Believe me, I wouldn't want to end the year thinking about how this year could have been better. No! The time to think about how this year could be better is RIGHT NOW! It's called planning, brainstorming, visioning, and sowing. Those things will infuse me with the mindset that it takes to achieve what I need to achieve. It'll show me what I need to work on and what areas I need to grow in.
>
> If you believe you are responsible for your success, you'll hustle hard every single day. You'll grind out the

work it takes to achieve your dreams no matter how difficult it can be. You'll follow through on every plan in spite of the temptation to quit on yourself because it's too hard. You'll invest in books and actually read them and more importantly, apply the wisdom from those books into your life. You'll pay whatever it takes to receive guidance and knowledge because you will reap what you sow. You'll keep convincing yourself that your dream-come-true moment is right around the corner no matter how long it takes.

Don't be a cheapskate. Pay the price. It will be worth it![7]

Everyone has inside of him a piece of good news. The good news is that you don't know how great you can be! How much you can love! What you can accomplish! And what your potential is!
—ANNE FRANK[8]

CAUTION: THERE MAY BE DETOURS ON THE ROAD TO SUCCESS

It is not uncommon to read about entrepreneurs who started like a ball of fire, only to fizzle out before reaching the finish line.

John Hamm, writing in *Harvard Business Review,* says,

> "It's a cliché to say that founders flounder, but unfortunately, that's usually the case. Wild exceptions like Bill Gates, Steve Jobs, and Michael Dell aside,

executives who start a business or project fizzle more often than not once they've gotten their venture on its feet." Hamm continues to explain that many "struggle to adapt as their companies grow beyond a handful of employees and launch a new product or service."[9]

Hamm details many obstacles that hinder the continued growth of start-up entrepreneurs. But my interpretation of his assessment is, "they didn't plan on any detours that might take them on another route to success!"

LET'S TALK ABOUT DETOURS...

What is a detour? Merriam-Webster defines a detour as a deviation from a direct course or the usual procedure: especially a round-about way temporarily replacing part of a route.[10]

A pastor friend of mine told me about the time he was to speak at a conference in Atlanta. Since the conference location was not that far from his home in Tennessee, he decided to drive. So, he and his son-in-law headed out on a bright, beautiful October day to take the three-hour journey. What could possibly go wrong?

He described what happened next:

> We were about midway to our destination when we started seeing the cars in front of us slowing down. We were traveling on one of the busiest interstate highways in America—so slowing down was not something we expected. You can imagine our shock when all traffic came to a complete standstill -no movement—nothing but frozen traffic as far as the eye could see. Finally, after about a half-hour wait, we were able to creep along

only to face a detour sign, with big flashing lights, telling us we would have to take an alternate route. The interstate was shut down due to a horrific accident, and we had to find another way to Atlanta. We took the next exit and found a state highway that eventually led us to the city. We finally made it to the conference through small towns, speed traps, and a hundred vegetable stands—just as I was being introduced. Our 3-hour trip took almost 6 hours. Now, that's a detour!

If you are willing to take the time and effort to become an overnight success (see Noah), you can be sure that detours are going to come your way.

Detours are going to happen even to the best-laid plans.

AND, WHEN A DETOUR HAPPENS, IT IS BEST TO REMEMBER:

The purpose of a detour is not to stop our journey but alert us that there may be trouble ahead. The issue is not "if" detours will happen, but how will you react when they do?

You could:

Turn around and go back home.

For some people, all it takes is one detour to dissuade them from continuing on their journey. Quitting seems to be the first choice, instead of trusting that God already knows what we are facing. A detour may be God's way of telling us there is a better route than the one we are on.

Blame others for the detour.

One of our favorite pastimes is to blame others when things don't go our way. Do you ever wonder why the guys who hold up the signs on highway construction sites look like they are not having a good time? They are probably responding to the adverse reactions of the motorists passing by!

Find another way.

I would imagine more than a few drivers who decided to find their route upon seeing a detour sign said, "This detour is nuts, and it will take too long. I'll find a better way!" There is an old saying that might apply that says, "It's always a safer bet to follow the signs instead of going your own way."

Ignore the detour signs and keep going into danger.

You don't have to be really smart to figure out that going around a detour sign may lead to danger. Whether we like them or not, detours exist for a reason. Finding out the hard way (by going around) why the detour is there in the first place is not a good strategy.

Apps like MapQuest, Google Maps, and others cannot possibly detail every detour, diversion, or bypass one might encounter. The most detailed plans in pursuing our dreams and God's best for our lives will have a few side trips along the way. Any of the reactions I have listed above will allow those detours to delay or even stifle our dreams.

America has been the breeding ground for many "overnight" success stories. There is one man who stands above the rest (for me at least). This man epitomizes the American success story—his name is Sam Walton.

Despite many detours and roadblocks, he persevered. A brief article published in Entrepreneur.com sums up how Sam Walton became an "overnight" success.

> Part P.T. Barnum, part Billy Graham, Sam Walton single-handedly built Wal-Mart into the biggest retailer in the world, transforming the way America shopped and making himself one of the world's richest men in the process. Thanks to his "aw, shucks" demeanor and his strategy of targeting rural areas, retailing giants like Kmart, Sears, and Woolworth's never saw the scrappy, pickup-driving country boy coming. And when they did, it was too late to stop him.
>
> Sam Walton didn't invent retailing, just like Henry Ford didn't invent the automobile. But just as Ford's assembly line revolutionized American industry, Walton's dogged pursuit of discounting revolutionized America's service economy. Walton didn't merely alter the way America shopped—he changed the philosophy of the American retail business establishment, instigating the shift of power from manufacturer to consumer that has become prevalent in industry after industry. His pioneering concepts paved the way for a new breed of "category killer" retailer—the Home Depots, Barnes & Nobles, and Blockbusters of the world—and forever changed the face of retailing.[11]
>
> Toward the end of his career Walton was asked by an interviewer what it felt like to be an overnight success? He said, "Well, I don't know if I would call twenty years overnight, but it does feel great!"[12]

ONE MORE THOUGHT...

It is better to understand that success is a journey and not a destination. Having understood *that* concept helps you to answer some very fundamental questions:

Who are your traveling companions?

Who you decide to take with you on your journey will greatly determine your level of success. When you are focused on your dream, there will usually be an exchange of personnel. Those who are going in the same direction will join up with you, and those who are not will fall by the wayside. Be prepared for both to happen.

What price are you willing to pay to complete your dream?

Noah was on a journey, and so are you. He knew it was going to take patience and perseverance to accomplish his goal. Despite all of the obstacles, Noah did not give up or give in to the temptation to quit. Noah was willing to pay any price to complete his assignment—and save mankind.

How will you handle the detours?

While it is true that detours are not cause for celebration, it's also true that detours are going to happen—no matter how much we try to avoid them. Detours, keep in mind, can either be self-imposed or God-ordained. It's vitally important that we identify the source and respond accordingly. The last thing we want to do is fail the "detour test" and start all over again. I learned a long time ago you do not flunk one of God's tests—you just get to do it over again—until you get it right! Coincidentally, Billie Kaye and

I have discovered some of the most beautiful scenery, unique restaurants and specialty shops because of detours. *Your detour could actually be a better way of getting to where you are going.*

Of course that was only after my attitude changed.

I'm sure you have heard the saying, "Rome wasn't built in a day." The meaning is clear—if you are going to build something that will last (your dream), it takes time and effort to get there. It also reminds us that although *"Rome wasn't built in a day, but they were laying bricks every hour!"* There is nothing fancy or newsworthy about laying brick. But, laying brick day by day, hour by hour, is how you get to the result—the Roman Empire.

Author Gary Keller said,

> Purpose is the straightest path to power and the ultimate source of personal strengths—strength of conviction, and strength to persevere. The prescription for extraordinary results is knowing what matters to you and taking daily doses of actions in alignment with it.[13]

I have a question. Do you want to become an overnight success? *Wonderful—now pick up another brick and keep building!*

ENDNOTES

1. Sam Walton, Wal-Mart founder. Quote taken from Good to Great by Jim Collins. https://www.forbes.com/sites/kensundheim/2013/12/12/10-inspiring-career-quotes-from-10-inspiring-authors/? Accessed March 31, 2021.

2. Curtis Jackson [50 Cent], American Rapper. From his interview with Louis Gannon for *Live* magazine, *The Mail on Sunday* (UK) newspaper, (25 October 2009) https://en.wikiquote.org/wiki/Success. Accessed April 1, 2021.

3. Sir Cameron Mackintosh British theater producer and businessman. From his interview with Martyn Lewis in Lewis' book, *Reflections on Success* (1997) https://en.wikiquote.org/wiki/Success. Accessed April 1, 2021.

4. James Richardson Vectors: Aphorisms and Ten Second Essays (2001), #135 https://en.wikiquote.org/wiki/Success. Accessed April 1, 2021.

5. Rick Warren, *The Purpose Driven Life: What on Earth Am I Here for?* https://www.goodreads.com/author/quotes/711.Rick_Warren. Accessed April 2, 2021.

6. https://www.merriam-webster.com/dictionary/potential. Accessed April 2, 2021.

7. Fredy Romero, "What is the price of Greatness?" http://www .fredyromero.com/blog/2016/1/20/what-is-the-price-of-greatness, Accessed April 2, 2021.

8. https://www.1001quotes.org/quote/anne-frank-87906. Accessed April 2, 2021.

9. John Hamm, "Why Entrepreneurs Don't Scale," *Harvard Business Review*, https://hbr.org/2002/12/why-entrepreneurs-dont-scale. Accessed April 4, 2021.

10. https://www.merriam-webster.com/dictionary/detour. Accessed April 4, 2021.

11. https://www.entrepreneur.com/article/197560. Accessed March 31, 2021.

12. https://rockerfeller.medium.com/sam-walton-of-wal-mart-fame-was -asked-in-an-interview-what-it-felt-like-to-be-an-overnight-success -286406ba47fa. Accessed April 6, 2021.

13. https://strategicdiscipline.positioningsystems.com/blog-0/purpose -the-dickens-of-your-one-thing. Accessed April 7, 2021.

6

DON'T LISTEN TO THE NON-DREAMERS

(Never Take Advice from Someone Who's Never Done Anything)

Always listen to experts. They'll tell you what can't be done and why. Then do it.

—ROBERT A. HEINLEIN[1]

For Christ also suffered once for sins, the righteous for the unrighteous, to bring you to God. He was put to death in the body but made alive in the Spirit. After being made alive he went and made proclamation to the imprisoned spirits—to those who were disobedient long ago when God waited patiently in the days of Noah while the ark was being built. In it only a few people, eight in all, were saved through water.

—1 PETER 3:18-20

For years, we have been told that Noah was constantly abused, mocked, and criticized for his efforts to save the planet. Many people thought that poor Noah worked from daylight to dark to finish the Ark while his neighbors were standing around making fun of him. That particular vision of Noah is not found in the Bible. Jesus said in Matthew 24:37-39,

> *As it was in the days of Noah, so it will be at the coming of the Son of Man. For in the days before the flood, people were eating and drinking, marrying and giving in marriage, up to the day Noah entered the ark; and they knew nothing about what would happen until the flood came and took them all away.*

Jesus (referring to Noah) made it perfectly clear—no one was giving Noah a second thought—*"they knew nothing about what would happen until the flood came and took them all away."*

But, we do have a few hints:

- Noah was a *"preacher of righteousness"* (2 Peter 2:5), who lived a blameless life (Genesis 6:9).
- It stands to reason that during the 100+ years it took to build the Ark, he took the time to preach God's Word to anyone who would listen.
- Warning people of impending judgment was in God's character, so it is not surprising that God would assign Noah the task of issuing a warning (see Jonah 3:4).
- Because people were surprised when the floods came, it did not mean that Noah refused to warn them.

While there is no scriptural evidence that Noah was mocked for his devotion, I can guarantee you that plenty of people were ready to offer advice and criticism of the construction project. How do I know that? Simple—it's called the *human condition*. Giving advice, offering criticism, and becoming an expert at almost everything is just a part of who we are as human beings.

James Thurber was a humorist, cartoonist, author, playwright, and journalist known for his quirky and relatable character and themes. He was one of the foremost American humorists of the 20th century.[2] Thurber once said, "*It is better to know some of the questions than all of the answers.*"[3] What did he mean by that quote? Is he saying that a person should never strive to know as much about a subject as possible? Is he saying that education is just a waste of time? If your son just turned sixteen and is about to take his driver's test, should you not get him the book provided by the DMV and help him study so he can know all the answers? Would it be more practical to let your son go in "blind" and just wing it? No, of course not.

Thurber was not referring to a driver's exam or any such thing. According to author Dennis LaMountain, *he is referring to people who take great pride in showing off how much they know—on almost all occasions! These are people who give answers at times in which asking questions would be more productive.*[4]

SIX TYPES OF NON-DREAMERS YOU SHOULD NOT ASK TO HELP YOU BUILD YOUR DREAM

1. *The Empty Suits.*

According to dictionary.com, an empty suit is "an executive, manager, or official regarded as ineffectual, incompetent, or lacking in leadership qualities such as creativity and empathy." In other words, an empty suit is someone who looks like they know what they are talking about, but when they open their mouth, it becomes apparent there isn't anything coming out but hot air!

Under the heading of "lessons, I learned the hard way," I have discovered that it's not wise to take "expert advice" from someone who has no accomplishments. Think about the last time you had a medical issue. Instead of going to the doctor to get a proper medical diagnosis, you instead decide to have a chat with the FedEx guy who just delivered a package to your door. Now, he may or may not know about medicine, but are you willing to take that chance? Yeah, that's what I thought—me neither. If it's all the same, I'll go to someone who has the training and experience and knows what they are talking about.

Not many of us have escaped the glaring eye of the "empty suit" as we try to find a more productive way to grow our organization or ministry. You know the ones who love to sit in judgment as we struggle to move to another level of success. They just are waiting for the right moment to swoop in and tell us how to do it better. One definition says an expert is, *"one who knows more and more about less and less until he knows absolutely everything about nothing."*[5]

2. The Dream Killers.

Who are the dream killers, you say? You know who they are— the negative people who will surround you and do all in their power to choke the life right out of you. They are the waterboys on your team, and as soon as they see you're getting hot, they will throw cold water in your face. They are weeds in your garden, and they need to be pulled out!

One lesson successful people have learned is this: If your circle of influence is not adding value to your dreams and goals, they will eventually suck the life out of you. It is vitally important to limit the amount of access the dream killers have in your life. Cutting access to the dream killers will enable you to limit the negativity they bring and enhance your ability to focus on the positive steps you need to take to fulfill your destiny. If you want to continue to rise to the next level of success, you need to determine who the life-givers are and who the life-takers are. The attitude of the dream killers is, "you will never accomplish anything worthwhile."

I have never met a dream killer who was not also a vocal critic, have you? An excellent example of how to handle the dream killers is the story of Colonel William Gorgas. He was in charge of building the Panama Canal. When he was asked by a New York Times reporter what he thought about those criticizing his construction project, he stayed quiet. After some time passed, the reporter pressed him for an answer. "Aren't you going to answer your critics?" Colonel Gorgas looked at him and said, "In time." Again, the reporter pressed for more clarity—"How?" With a smile, Gorgas said, "With the canal." His answer to the naysayers came on August 15, 1914. The Panama Canal opened for shipping for the first time. His attitude was apparent—I will answer the dream killers by what I do, not by what I say!

It was Ray Goforth who said, *"there are two types of people who will tell you that you cannot make a difference in this world: those who are afraid to try and those who are afraid you will succeed."*[6]

3. The Do-Nothings.

I'm sure you have met the "do-nothings" before. The do-nothings are the ones who are NOT doing anything to accomplish their dreams, and they get upset with you when they see you are not willing to join the do-nothing club with them. Their motto is simple: "We are not doing anything, and we want you to join our club and do nothing with us!" THESE PEOPLE DRIVE ME UP A WALL.

Asking a person with no experience in starting, running, or growing any business is a dangerous proposition. Why? If they don't have any knowledge or successful history that will make a difference, then whatever counsel they offer is nothing more than opinion. Staying at a Holiday Inn Express does not qualify as the necessary experience to guide you on your journey.

A particular story in the Bible perfectly illustrates what happens when you turn to the do-nothings for counsel.

The story is found in First Kings 12 and is about a young king named Rehoboam. After his father, King Solomon, died, he needed counsel on how to govern the people. The people had asked if he would consider lifting the heavy burden imposed by his father. Rehoboam found himself in a unique position. He had to choose between two groups of counselors. On one side were the men who served with his father. Their counsel was very wise, birthed out of years of experience. You might say they had been around the block a time or two on this whole governing thing. They said it would be prudent to consent to the people and give them what they asked for.

> *If today you will be a servant to these people and serve them and give them a favorable answer, they will always be your servants* (1 Kings 12:7).

On the other side was the second group of men who were his buddies. These guys grew up with the young king. You might say (in modern language) this was his posse. But, they had no experience in such matters. Not only did their counsel reveal a more sinister agenda, but it also revealed their total lack of concern to help the young king become revered by his subjects.

> *The young men who had grown up with him replied,*
> *"These people have said to you, 'Your father put a heavy*
> *yoke on us, but make our yoke lighter.' Now tell them,*
> *'My little finger is thicker than my father's waist. My*
> *father laid on you a heavy yoke; I will make it even*
> *heavier. My father scourged you with whips; I will*
> *scourge you with scorpions'"* (1 Kings 12:10-11).

Unfortunately for the king (and the people), he made a bad decision. He listened to the wrong counsel given by the do-nothings, and it had disastrous consequences. His success was severely hindered. (You can read the complete account in 1 Kings 12-13).

It was a hard lesson for the king to learn, and we would be wise to learn from his mistake. Be very careful when getting advice on how to rise to new heights from those who have never been where you want to go!

4. Your BFF.

Happy is the person who has a BFF (Best Friend Forever). We all need friends in our life, and to have a small circle of close friends is a blessing. But, as important as friends are, we must be careful when receiving counsel solely based on friendship.

Friends can be great people to go to for advice, but only if they are willing to be honest with you. The best of friends are the ones that aren't afraid to tell you the truth, even if it isn't what you want to hear. And, they know how to do it in a nice way. Chances are, you know where your friends fall on the spectrum. If a friend only tells you what you want to hear, it doesn't necessarily mean they aren't a good friend, but they aren't the right friend to ask for advice.[7]

The right associations will always bring out the best in you. It's critical with whom you closely associate. Remember, the devil will never use strangers to stop your progress toward your destiny. Wrong associations will always bring out the worst in you. I am sure you've noticed that when you hang around positive faith-filled people, you find yourself more excited, less critical, and possess a clearer vision of the future. After spending time with negative people, you find yourself full of doubt, fear, confusion, and criticism.

A very wise man once said, *"I can always tell what you like by the friends that you keep. You will always attract what you are."* I can predict your future by looking at your friends. Where they are, is where you're headed. If you want to remove negative prophecies from your life, you should remove negative people from your life. You will discover that some friends will leave your life with each new level of assignment, and new ones will enter.

If you want to position yourself to live a more purposeful life, find friends who do what you want to do. Find friends who are going where you want to go; then you can go there together. It's a fantastic concept; you can alter your future by changing your friends.

An old leadership proverb states, "Be with people who will celebrate you, and not tolerate you." In each week (7 days), there are 10,080 minutes; having a lack of time is not the problem, but having a sense of direction and using your time wisely are critical factors.

Your success is determined by those whom you let have access to those minutes. When you study the secrets of successful people, you discover they control who enjoys access to their time. The greatest treasure you can give someone is access. People who do not respect your time will not appreciate your wisdom. If you are not careful, you will let wrong priorities and the wrong people consume your time.

Paul told his protégé Timothy to take the things he had seen, the teachings he had heard, and pass them on to a reliable man that would teach others. In other words, only give what I've given you to people that are going to be producers. Access is the only influence that you have in your life. Proverbs 12:26 *says, "The righteous choose their friends carefully, but the way of the wicked leads them astray."*

5. The Experts (non-dreamers).

Don't misunderstand. I'm not suggesting that all "experts" are just out for the money and don't care about results. I don't rule out the fact that I should ask someone for help or get advice by those who may happen to have more knowledge about a subject than I do. When seeking advice, it's always helpful to remember that the ark was built by amateurs, while the Titanic by professionals!

Many problems arise because we are looking for an easy way out instead of doing the heavy lifting ourselves. A 20-year study of political experts done by Philip Tetlock, *found that their predictions were no better than flipping a coin. Further, he found that pundits who specialized in a particular field tended to perform worse than those whose knowledge was more general.*[8]

Want proof?

Consider the case of the New Coke disaster.

One of the most glaring miscalculations that consultants, experts, (and those who should have known better) occurred during the months of April-May 1985. It has been deemed one of the colossal business failures of modern times. It happened to the Coca-Cola company. It's hard to imagine that this nightmare happened under the skillful eye of its president, Donald R. Keough—but it did.

In his book, *The Ten Commandments for Business Failure,* Keough recounts the time that he and his management team listened to the so-called experts (non-dreamers), and acting on the advice of those "experts," almost sank one of the most successful companies in American history.

> When the management of Coca-Cola USA came to corporate leadership with a New Coke proposal, we were persuaded to take a serious look. This was the case when Roberto and I allowed ourselves to be convinced by consultants and experts that the huge number of taste tests conducted by the U.S. market research group provided us with a valid basis to make the move to an entirely new product formation. After weeks of reviews, debate, and discussion, Roberto and I supported the project. They had convinced us that changing the product would be a brilliant competitive move.
>
> Almost immediately after the announcement, complaints tied up the phone circuits to Atlanta in ever-increasing numbers of telephone calls. In a matter of a few weeks, we had more than four hundred thousand letters and calls—all negative. Our experts urged

us to stay the course. Our research gurus and marketing experts told us it was just a matter of time. New Coke was going to be a smash success. All the complaints are just keeping the Coke name in the press.

It became crystal clear that we were not dealing with a taste issue or any real marketing issue. All the experts and all their data had been misleading. This was a deep psychological issue. A brand is not defined by what you or I think it is. A brand is defined by what is embedded in the mind of each consumer. The U.S. consumer had spoken clearly and loudly: Coca-Cola was their product, and they wanted it back. We agreed.

Keough added: Meanwhile, the experts who helped us into this situation went on their way to "help" other people. Whatever happened to common sense? The expertise of some experts had been disproved so many times that you would think they would wear out their welcome.[9]

New Coke was out, and Coke Classic old Coke was back in—and the rest, as they say, is history!

6. The Woodpeckers.

Dealing with woodpeckers is a real challenge. They are very subtle but steady at their work. Your dream is an indictment against their mundane, dull, dry life. And so they peck away at yours. "You can't do it. No one can build that business. You're wasting your time. I know someone who had a similar dream and they failed." On and on they peck away at your dream. They have to because they've already sunk their ark. Don't let them peck away at yours. Your family's future, like Noah's, depends on it.

ONE MORE THOUGHT...

It may sound a tad simplistic, but my life experience has taught me that there are two ways to learn, *by mistakes or mentors, and not necessarily the experts.* I highly suggest a mentor. A mentor is someone who has been (or is going) where you want to go. They may not be building the same boat (destiny) that you are building, but that doesn't mean their input is invalid. A trusted mentor will have the knowledge and wisdom you need that will keep you from making disastrous decisions. Just because everyone in the room thinks something is a good idea does not mean that it is—think New Coke.

King Solomon, who was one of the wisest and richest men who ever lived, advocated for wise counsel. He said in Proverbs 11:14, *"for lack of guidance a nation falls, but victory is won through many advisers"* And, again in Proverbs 15:22, *"Plans fail for lack of counsel, but with many advisers they succeed."*

Solomon also reminded us that those from whom you choose to receive counsel, make all the difference. Your success or failure is in your hand by who has your ear. Proverbs 13:20, *"Walk with the wise and become wise, for a companion of fools suffers harm."* There is a big difference between having a close friend and a mentor. Your friends are happy with the way you are, but a mentor loves you too much to allow you to remain in your current condition. A mentor is more concerned about your progress than a friend who simply acts as a cheerleader.

Cheerleaders are wonderful, but coaches win games!

ENDNOTES

1. https://www.ranker.com/list/notable-and-famous-experts-quotes/
    reference. Accessed April 13, 2021.

2. https://www.thurberhouse.org/james-thurber. Accessed April 13,
    2021.

3. https://lamountaincoaching.com/communication/better-know
    -questions-answers/. Accessed April 13, 2021.

4. Ibid. Accessed April 13, 2021.

5. http://rudyh.org/dictionary-fun-funny-quotes-quotations.htm.
    Accessed April 13, 2021.

6. https://www.wisesayings.com/negative-people-quotes/
    #ixzz6u5wwMYgI. Accessed April 14, 2021.

7. http://stuckinyourrut.com/about/ Accessed April 14, 2021.

8. Greg Satell, "Why Experts Always Seem to Get It Wrong," https://
    www.forbes.com/sites/gregsatell/2014/02/19/why-experts-always-
    seem-to-get-it-wrong/?sh=673321f63a36. Accessed April 2, 2021.

9. Donald R. Keough, *The Ten Commandments for Business Failure*.
    (New York, NY: Penguin Group, 2008, 2011). p. 104-107.

7

FOLLOW THE BLUEPRINTS

(Don't Make It up as You Go!)

A successful man is one who can lay a firm foundation with the bricks others have thrown at him.

—DAVID BRINKLEY[1]

By the grace God has given me, I laid a foundation as a wise builder, and someone else is building on it. But each one should build with care. For no one can lay any foundation other than the one already laid, which is Jesus Christ.

—1 CORINTHIANS 3:10-11

The decision was made.

All humans were going to be wiped out, with a few notable exceptions.

And now, the only decision left was who could God trust with such a vast undertaking. You might imagine that God looked everything over and found one man was worthy—his name was

Noah. *"But Noah found favor in the eyes of the Lord. This is the account of Noah and his family. Noah was a righteous man, blameless among the people of his time, and he walked faithfully with God"* (Genesis 6:8-9).

But, keep in mind one thing.

Noah didn't volunteer for the job.

Noah wasn't sitting around reading the latest leadership manual and suddenly decided to throw his hat in the ring to lead such a massive construction project—quite the contrary. Noah found himself in one of those "good new-bad news" situations. The good news was he found favor with God—the bad news was he was *called* to build the world's largest floating box, and save the earth. Noah might have thought, "I don't think I can handle any more good news!"

As I previously noted (in chapter 4), the only thing Noah had was a specific set of building plans, and he was not to deviate from those plans—not one inch. Without any help (not even a Time-Life book), Noah did exactly what the instructions said to do.

The details are found in Genesis 6:14-21: Use cypress wood, make rooms or divisions in it (so, for example, the foxes can't get to the chickens); coat it with pitch inside and out. Make the dimensions 300 cubits long, fifty cubits wide and thirty cubits high. (Since it's going to rain like crazy), and make a roof, but leave an opening all around the arc under the roof one cubit high (Trust me, you'll need fresh air). Make three-story decks and make a nice wide door—the elephants are pretty hefty. Bring in male and female of everything that flies, walks or scurries and enough food of all kinds (the tigers and lions like theirs fresh and moving) to be stored for the animals and for you. Noah, I know it's a ton of work, but you need to get it done—it's going to rain soon—and you don't want to get caught unprepared!

Why was Noah a successful leader?

Noah did what God told him to do. He paid attention to the plans and didn't deviate from the strategy.

Each time Noah was given the instructions, he obeyed (see Genesis 6:22—7:5). Noah was not only willing to build this "floating box" as instructed, but he was willing to build EXACTLY as he was instructed. His family's future, the animals, and all future generations depended on the preciseness of his obedience!

Strategies for success are not necessarily confined to just a few of the highly motivated or for those who have a "knack" for doing it right the first time.

After years of up-close and personal observation of successful leaders, I have come to realize that:

- Successful leaders come in all shapes and sizes. Leadership is not a one size fits all approach.
- Successful leaders possess a common behavior pattern in life and work.
- Successful leaders derive their strategy from different sources, i.e., family, mentors, seeking, spiritual awakening, disaster, and even the entertainment industry, etc.
- Successful leaders are willing to learn strategies that work in every circumstance.
- Successful leaders are not afraid to fail.
- Successful leaders do not have a "my way or the highway" strategy for success.

Eleanor Roosevelt once remarked, "A good leader inspires people to have confidence in the leader, a great leader inspires people to have confidence in themselves."[2]

3 STRATEGIES FOR SUCCESS THAT YOU CAN TAKE TO THE BANK

Strategy #1—Build a Solid Foundation.

Whether you are building a twenty-thousand square foot mansion, or a shed to house your lawnmower, the foundation must be built first. Load-bearing walls must have a foundation to stand on or the building will collapse. David Allan Coe once remarked: It is not the beauty of a building you should look at; it's the construction of the foundation that will stand the test of time.[3]

Noah is a prime example of what healthy leadership looks like. After reading his story, you begin to see the ingredients of a solid foundation.

- Responsible: When God called Noah to the task, he did not shirk his responsibility.
- Obedient: He set the example for all leaders by following the instructions and never wavering from the assigned blueprints.
- Visionary: Throughout the project (of building the Ark), he maintained his vision.
- Servant: He was a servant leader.
- Persistent: He understood that nothing worthwhile is completed overnight.
- Integrity: Noah's backbone and discipline demonstrated his inward strength.

There are plenty of other examples in the Bible of godly leadership besides Noah; Jesus, Paul, and Simon Peter come immediately to mind. It would be beneficial to your leadership development to study these and others to understand better what godly leadership looks like. Suffice it to say that if we claim to be followers of Christ, then a solid, spiritual foundation is essential. The apostle Paul said it best, *"For no one can lay any foundation other than the one already laid, which is Jesus Christ"* (1 Corinthians 3:11).

> *Do you wish to be great? Then begin by being. Do you desire to construct a vast and lofty fabric? Think first about the foundations of humility. The higher your structure is to be, the deeper must be its foundation.*
> —ST. AUGUSTINE OF HIPPO (354-430)[4]

Strategy #2—Take Out Your Shovel and Start Digging.

I believe that God has implanted in our DNA two powerful forces: *gifting and passion.* These undeniable qualities are not there for entertainment or personal enjoyment. They are there to bring out the treasure implanted in you, (by your creator), to the visible world.

The apostle Paul encouraged the saints to *"work out your salvation with fear and trembling."*

> *Therefore, my dear friends, as you have always obeyed—not only in my presence, but now much more in my absence—continue to work out your salvation with fear and trembling, for it is God who works in you to will and to act in order to fulfill his good purpose* (Philippians 2:12).

Paul told the Philippians (and us) to *"dig deep"* to discover the beautiful treasures that God planted within each one of them!

DREAMS Everything you see in the visible world first started deep in the heart of someone who combined discipline and passion along with hard work to make it happen. The next time you think about Noah and his Ark, understand it did not become a reality when the first load of cypress wood was dropped off at the construction site. It started in the heart and the soul of this man who "saw" the Ark on the inside before it was manifest on the outside.

Phillips Brooks (1835-1893) observed:

> Dreadful will be the day when the world becomes contented when one great universal satisfaction spreads itself over the world. Sad will be the day for every man when he becomes absolutely contented with the life that he is living, with the thoughts that he is thinking, with the deeds that he is doing, when there is not forever beating at the doors of his soul some great desire to do something larger which he knows that he was meant and made to do because he is a child of God.[5]

What about you?

Are you digging for spiritual gold?

If You Want to Be a Successful "Gold-Digger," You Must NOT...

- Discount your dreams. For every invention or new strategy to improve our lives, there is a list of people who first dreamed it before it became a reality.

- Be afraid to take small steps to develop the hidden treasure of the heart. A successful future is often determined by your daily habits. Remember, WHO you become TOMORROW begins with what you do TODAY!

- Push away mentors from your life. A mistake will teach you not to run into the ditch again, but a mentor will teach you how to avoid the ditch altogether!

- Allow negative feelings to convince you that "it can't be done." Successful leaders are no different than anyone else when it comes to dealing with negative influences. The overriding difference between the successful and the unsuccessful is, they choose to refuse to back down. The WILL to overcome when the odds are not in their favor is what pushes them to success.

- Forget to ask the One who created you to help you find your heart, mind, soul, and the treasures He has placed there for you.

Deep within man dwell those slumbering powers; powers that would astonish him, that he never dreamed of possessing; forces that would revolutionize his life if aroused and put into action.
—ORISON MARDEN[6]

Each of us has the same choice. We can choose to refuse difficult circumstances, fears, and obstacles and to bury the hidden treasure in our hearts. Our number one priority is to "dig up" and live out our potential.

Strategy #3—Look on the Bright Side.

Looking on the *bright side* does not imply that we ignore the negative things that swirl around us. A simple definition from-macmillandictionary.com says that *bright side* thinking is *"to think about the good parts of a situation that is mostly bad."*

Wishing and hoping that negative things never happen is not a strategy for success. Why? Hiding under the bed will not make the negative go away—it only delays the obvious—negative things do happen to *bright-side* thinkers, and we must be prepared to deal with them.

Dr. Henry Cloud, in his book, *9 Things a Leader Must Do,* stated:

> If there is no hope for whatever it is you are clinging to, let go of it so you can be open to something new and life-giving. New things that actually have hope for the future cannot appear until you get rid of what was taking up the space that the new thing needs.[7]

Did you know that negative thinking can affect your brain, and in turn, affect your physical and emotional health?

According to research done at King's College London, negative thinking may increase the risk of someone getting Alzheimer's disease.

> The study found that a habit of prolonged negative thinking diminishes your brain's ability to think, reason, and form memories. Essentially draining

your brain's resources. Another study reported in the journal American Academy of Neurology found that cynical thinking also produces a greater dementia risk.[8]

Several years ago, *Guideposts* posted excerpts from *The Power of Positive Thinking* by the greatest bright side thinker that ever penned a manuscript, Dr. Norman Vincent Peale.

Below is my analysis of three of my favorites points from Dr. Peale.

1. Affirm All is Possible. Luke 18:27, Jesus replied, *"What is impossible with man is possible with God."* I don't think Dr. Peale is saying that we should take our hands off a seemingly impossible situation and allow God to do everything for us. It seems every time I ask God to remove an impossible situation, He gives an instruction on how to participate in my miracle. "Affirming All is Possible" with God means our faith and hope are rooted in God's promise that *"we know that in all things God works for the good of those who love him, who have been called according to his purpose"* (Romans 8:28). Don't run from an impossible situation; run to the God who can do above our wildest imagination.

2. Expect Good Things. Psalm 62:5, *"Yes, my soul, find rest in God; my hope comes from him."* Many people live with a sky-is-falling approach to life. No matter how many good things happen, they will almost always expect something bad to follow. Always waiting for the other shoe to drop is a terrible way to live.

God's people have every right to expect favor to follow after them because they have royal blood flowing through their veins. Every farmer knows that between planting and harvesting is a season of expectation. Because the farmer has worked the soil and planted, he has every expectation that something good will come up out of the ground. As believers, we build our expectations, not by wishful thinking, but a hope built on the foundation of God's word.

3. Trust with All Your Heart. Proverbs 3:5-6, *"Trust in the Lord with all your heart and lean not on your own understanding; in all your ways submit to him, and he will make your paths straight."* Trust in the Lord is not only a wise thing to do, but it is a shelter in a time of a storm. When our desires line up with His desires, we find a sense of peace and contentment that cannot be found in worldly pleasures. The psalmist declared the same sentiment when he proclaimed, *"Trust in the Lord and do good; dwell in the land and enjoy safe pasture. Take delight in the Lord, and he will give you the desires of your heart. Commit your way to the Lord; trust in him and he will do this: He will make your righteous reward shine like the dawn, your vindication like the noonday sun"* (Psalm 37:3-6).[9]

When tragic circumstances blow an unexpected wind into our lives (without an invitation), we are often left with a tremendous challenge: how can anyone look on the *bright side* of this circumstance?

Below is the true story of how a Southern Baptist missionary named Gloria Sloan faced an unspeakable tragedy.

On June 18, 1999, Gary and Gloria Sloan, Southern Baptist missionaries, who had been on the field of Mexico only six months, were enjoying a birthday celebration for their daughter, Carla, at a popular swimming spot on Mexico's Pacific coast. With them were two other young missionaries from the United States, Joy Murphy and John Weems.

Due to a strong undertow, Carla began to be pulled out to sea. Gary Sloan and the other two missionaries rushed to save eleven-year-old Carla, but were overcome and drowned, as did she.

When Carla's body was brought to shore, Gloria doubled over in agony, unable to breathe. But it was then that she felt the physical presence of Jesus. Gloria said, "I felt such a strength and power and control. I looked down at my daughter, and I had such a peace."

...A large group of people gathered to watch this unfolding tragedy. And before long, four bodies lay in the sand. But what happened next is truly amazing. Gloria stood over the bodies of her dead loved ones and gave witness to the saving power of Christ. She told the people, "The pain I felt because of the loss of my husband and daughter was not as much pain as I felt for the true lost-ness of those standing around me" (The Commission, a publication of the International Missions Board of the Southern Baptist Convention, pg. 29).[10]

I pray that you will never have to face such a horrible situation as Gloria Sloan, but know that we are not left alone in our grief in our darkest hour. Our Heavenly Father will wrap us up in His loving embrace.

ONE MORE THOUGHT...

One of the most popular subjects for discussion these days is "What is leadership?" In this chapter, we highlighted Noah and mentioned others such as Jesus and the apostle Paul. But, let's face it, in today's culture, everyone has an opinion about the matter. Some say that certain leaders were born to be great; others say that great leaders are simply made out of whole cloth, based on environmental circumstances, good education, and the right opportunities.

I love what Supreme Court Justice Potter Stewart said in a case (Jacobellis v. Ohio) involving whether a movie was considered pornography or just good art. His opinion on the subject ended with this classic line...

> I shall not today attempt further to define the kinds of material I understand to be embraced within that shorthand description (hard-core pornography); and perhaps I could never succeed in intelligibly doing so. But I know it when I see it, and the motion picture involved in this case is not that.[11]

So, which is it?

Are leaders made or born?

Whatever side you come down on, one thing is true—successful leaders share common traits that are identifiable and reproducible. Characteristics such as a sense of purpose, consistent communication with the team, belonging to a higher purpose, and a resolve to get the job done are just a few of the dynamics that make up a successful leader.

Believe me. You will know it, when you see it!

ENDNOTES

1. https://www.azquotes.com/quote/36378. Accessed May 1, 2021.

2. https://www.leadership-central.com/famous-leadership-quotes.html. Accessed May 2, 2021.

3. https://www.supanet.com/find/famous-quotes-by/david-allan-coe/ it-is-not-the-beauty-of-a-fqb3390/. Accessed May 2, 2021.

4. https://www.brianhousand.com/blog/structure-curious-quotes. Accessed May 2, 2021.

5. Phillips Brooks, *Daily Thoughts from Phillips Brooks* (1893), p. 85. https://en.wikiquote.org/wiki/Motivation. Accessed May 2, 2021.

6. https://beyondthezonespirit.wordpress.com/2014/05/09/deep -within-man-dwell-those-slumbering-powers-powers-that-would -astonish-him-that-he-never-dreamed-of-possessing-forces-that -would-revolutionize-his-life-if-aroused-and-put-into-action/. Accessed May 4, 2021.

7. Dr. Henry Cloud, *9 Things a Leader Must Do,* (Nashville, TN: Thomas Nelson, 2006). p. 36.

8. https://www.bccpa.ca/news-events/latest-news/2018/is-negative -thinking-bad-for-your-brain/. Accessed May 5, 2021

9. I've only listed 3 of my favorite points from the article. I recommend reading the entire article: "8 Life-Changing Tips from 'The Power of Positive Thinking,'" by Dr. Norman Vincent Peale @ https://www .guideposts.org/better-living/8-life-changing-tips-from-the-power-of -positive-thinking. Accessed May 5, 2021.

10. This true story has been reported on by Baptist Press and many other SBC Missions organizations. But a more condensed version is found here from a sermon illustration by Pastor Donnie Martin. He reflects on the power of faith in the face of immense tragedy. Visit https://www.sermoncentral.com/sermon-illustrations/16783/thank-god-not-everyone-lets-the-negatives-of-by-donnie-martin. Accessed May 7, 2021.

11. Justice Potter Stewart, Concurring, Jacobellis v. Ohio, 378 U.S. 184 (1964). https://en.wikiquote.org/wiki/Potter_Stewart. Accessed May 7, 2021.

8

STAY SHIPSHAPE

(Don't Lose Your Dream So Close to the Finish Line)

Today I will do what others won't, so tomorrow I can accomplish what others can't.

—JERRY RICE[1]

In the six hundredth year of Noah's life, on the seventeenth day of the second month—on that day all the springs of the great deep burst forth, and the floodgates of the heavens were opened. And rain fell on the earth forty days and forty nights. On that very day Noah and his sons, Shem, Ham and Japheth, together with his wife and the wives of his three sons, entered the ark.

—GENESIS 7:11-13

Shipshape is a nautical term meaning in good and seamanlike order with reference to the condition of a ship. The expression had its origin when Bristol was the major west coast port of Britain at a time when all its shipping was maintained in good order. It can also mean: "trim, tidy, neat and with everything in its correct place."[2]

We can all agree that it is essential to maintain and keep in proper order your watercraft. If you want your voyage to be successful, don't neglect the very thing that will get you there.

It's imperative to keep your boat and everyone on it in shipshape!

Keeping things shipshape by no means exempts us from facing unexpected storms. Whether you are the captain of a large ship or a dingy, it's important to make sure that everything and everyone is in proper working condition—in other words, staying shipshape will keep you on course for a successful journey.

No one is ever fully prepared for the perfect storm, but as Tony O'Driscoll observed:

> In navigating the open seas—both stormy and calm—experienced captains focus on ensuring that everything remains shipshape. Daily drills are carried out to ensure that the crew practices their respective roles and responsibilities until they become second nature. In an organizational context, staying shipshape is analogous to "work routines and practices." The challenge our modern-day captains must confront is: "How do I implement work routines and practices that enable the organization to rapidly respond to uncertainty with competence and confidence?"[3]

One might conclude that piloting a large floating box (think captain Noah and his Ark) is *analogous* to you leading and guiding your organization, ministry, or family relationships.

This chapter is NOT simply talking about the proper care and maintenance of a ship, but also emphasizes keeping and maintaining in proper working condition a *living vessel*—YOU! Second Timothy 2:20-21 tells us,

> *In a large house there are articles not only of gold and silver, but also of wood and clay; some are for special purposes and some for common use. Those who cleanse themselves from the latter will be instruments for special purposes, made holy, useful to the Master and prepared to do any good work.*

Eleanor Roosevelt once said: "The purpose of life, after all, is to live it, to taste experience to the utmost, to reach out eagerly and without fear for newer and richer experiences."[4] Eleanor's sentiment is well taken, but to "reach out eagerly and without fear for newer and richer experiences" one must be willing to prepare in certain ways that will ensure a rewarding and pleasant journey.

3 TRAINING TOOLS THAT WILL HELP KEEP YOU SHIPSHAPE

Tool #1—Get Physical.

Do you remember the first time you watched a tightrope walker? You may have caught the act at a circus or watched it on television. Who can deny that the tension can be just as palpable for those watching as those walking on a tightrope hundreds of feet in the air?

One skill is demanded above all else—if you are going to walk a tightrope, you better have good balance or fall—and possibly die. Even the father of tightrope walkers, Karl Wallenda, was not immune to the danger of NOT maintaining proper balance.

I remember watching the news account of how Karl Wallenda fell during an attempted high-wire walk between two towers in San Juan, Puerto Rico.

The news report stated:

> Karl Wallenda had been performing stunts since he was six years old. He was trained to walk on a high wire, cycle across a tightrope, and balance as one of a seven-man pyramid. Rarely was a safety net used. For him, it seemed, nothing was impossible. Then, on March 22, 1978, the world watched in horror as Karl Wallenda fell to his death. As he attempted to walk across a high wire strung between the two towers of the Condado Plaza Hotel in San Juan, Puerto Rico, the 73-year-old Wallenda lost his balance, teetering on the wire for 30 heart-stopping seconds before plummeting 10 stories.
>
> Karl Wallenda's death might not have been so highly publicized had it not been for his daredevil reputation and the fact that it was broadcast live on television. About halfway across the wire he can be seen struggling with his balance and then falling. He struck a parked taxi and was pronounced dead. A later investigation revealed that a combination of high winds and the fact that the wire had been improperly secured was what led to Wallenda's tragic death.[5]

One might conclude that Wallenda's death might have been avoided. If the wire had been shipshape to allow Wallenda to maintain a better balance, the outcome would have been different.

In the case of Wallenda, his physical body vessel was older and weaker—more susceptible to imbalance, and his preparation was not thorough because his rope was not secured properly.

How many times have we been told how important it is to maintain balance in our lives? I doubt anyone (with half a brain) would advocate that we live our lives on the edge of extremes. Whether we want to admit it or not, we know that too much of anything, even good things, can cause harm—physically, mentally, and spiritually.

When I talk about physical balance, I'm not suggesting you learn how to balance on a tightrope. NO, I am talking about getting your body shipshape to be strong enough to carry you to the end of your journey. Don't be like the editorial columnist Billy Noonan (who was seventy years old at the time) who said to a group of fellow journalists who praised him, *"If I'd known I was going to live so long, I would have taken better care of myself!"*[6]

The apostle Paul said, *"have nothing to do with godless myths and old wives' tales; rather, train yourself to be godly. For physical training is of some value, but godliness has value for all things, holding promise for both the present life and the life to come"* (1 Timothy 4:7-8). Paul also said, *"Therefore I do not run like someone running aimlessly; I do not fight like a boxer beating the air. No, I strike a blow to my body and make it my slave so that after I have preached to others, I myself will not be disqualified for the prize"* (1 Corinthians 9:26-27).

Having a desire to get shipshape physically is one thing—achieving the goal is something altogether different. When it comes to getting in shape, I don't know how many New Year's resolutions have been made, only to be broken by the third week of

January. Why is that? It could be because it's much easier to talk about something (like weight loss) than actually getting off the couch and doing something!

At the ranch, we set up a very well-equipped workout room. Why? Because I know the importance of keeping myself in the best shape possible. Are there times when I don't even want to walk into the workout room? Yes, without a doubt. There are times when I would rather sit in a big comfy chair and watch a movie. But I know neglecting my physical body will eventually cost me—and I'm not willing to fall off the tightrope of sound physical health.

Stacy Reaoch offered this challenge:

> That exercise offers a mountain of benefits, from keeping our hearts pumping and muscles strong, to increasing our energy levels, to providing emotional highs that come from the release of endorphins. She adds this interesting insight; And when my body is not dragging me down, I find it less difficult to delight myself in the Lord. Exercise has a way of clearing the cobwebs from my brain and helping to hold my focus on the promises of Scripture.[7]

Tool #2—Take Small Steps.

Zechariah 4:10 says,

> *Who dares despise the day of small things, since the seven eyes of the Lord that range throughout the earth will rejoice when they see the chosen capstone in the hand of Zerubbabel?*

Small things have a way of turning into big things IF we don't give up. Small things can also equal big rewards if we are willing to understand that finding true purpose in life is not ONE big event—it's an accumulation of "small things" that turn into BIG things.

For instance, did you know that... *Compound Effect*

- Reading 20 pages per day is 30 books (on average length) per year.
- Saving $10 per day is $3,650 per year.
- Running 1 mile per day is 365 miles per year.
- Becoming 1% better per day is 37 times better per year.
- Little things are underestimated! (Unknown author)

There was once a struggling English teacher named Stephen. He fashioned himself to be a novelist, but as the rejections piled up, he knew that unless something changed, he would be forever doomed to insignificance. His life wasn't working out as he had planned. In 1973, Stephen wrote a few pages of what would become his first novel, *Carrie*—then decided it was no good and threw it away. Fortunately, his wife, Tabitha, found the pages in the trashcan of the couple's then broken-down double-wide, and convinced him otherwise. In his memoir *On Writing*, King quotes her as saying, "You've got something here. I really think you do, and you should finish it!" It turns out she was right. The book sold more than 1 million copies in its first year. It was also King's first big-screen film adaptation. That story, written by a 26-year-old teacher and laundry worker and published for the first time on April 5, 1974, would go on to transform King's life. Paperback rights sold for $400,000 to Signet Books, and the book itself "shook the horror field up like a bomb," says Ramsey Campbell, one of Britain's most respected horror writers. With millions of copies sold today, *Carrie* also launched the career of one of the world's bestselling novelist—his name is Stephen King.[8]

To find success or achieve your dreams you don't always have to do impossible, extraordinary, superhuman things. But, to understand what God intended for you to see, you must do something—so, start with what's in your hand.

> *Everything big starts with something small.*
> *All God needs is something to start with.*
>
> —JENTEZEN FRANKLIN

The Bible tells us that God can use the smallest, even the most insignificant of things to show forth His glory. It is never the size but the commitment to allow God to use what's in your hand that makes the difference.

- It was five small rocks that David picked up to defeat Goliath (1 Samuel 17:40).

- It was an insignificant rod in the hand of Moses that was transformed into the "rod of God" that led a nation out of bondage (Exodus 4:1-5).

- It was just a jawbone of a donkey that Samson picked up to use to kill a thousand Philistines (Judges 15:15).

- It was a lunch of five loaves and two small fish that was placed in the hand of Jesus that fed the multitude (John 6:1-14).

- It was a widow who dropped two small coins in the offering that got the attention and praise of Jesus (Mark 12:42).

- To save mankind from sin, God sent a baby named Jesus—such a small insignificant thing turned into the salvation for all who will receive Him (John 3:16).

- According to Jesus, the tiny mustard seed (one of the world's smallest seeds) can grow into a small tree that can provide nests for birds and shade from the heat (Matthew 13:31–32).

Did you know that the first step in building a bridge over Niagara Falls started with a 15-year-old boy and a kite? His name was Homan Walsh, and what he did with a small thing transformed that part of the world.

On January 30, 1848, Homan flew a kite he named Union from one side of the gorge to the other. Someone on the opposite side caught the kite and tied a stronger string to the end of the kite string, and Holman pulled the new, thicker string back across the gorge. The process was repeated with an even stronger string, then a cord, then a thin rope, then a thicker rope, and eventually a steel cable, which crossed the expanse and was strong enough to support workers, tools, and materials. Finally, a sturdy bridge, over which trains and trucks could easily pass, was completed. And it all began with a string.[9]

Jesus said, *"Whoever can be trusted with very little can also be trusted with much, and whoever is dishonest with very little will also be dishonest with much"* (Luke 16:10).

Tool #3—Finish Strong.

NICOVE

How is it possible to maintain the energy and drive to finish strong? After all, no one is immune from failure, setbacks, and challenges along the way. Proverbs 24:16 tells us, *"for though the righteous fall seven times, they rise again, but the wicked stumble when calamity strikes."* STUMBLE - LET BACK UP - TAKE NOS

If you desire to be a strong finisher, then you must "become someone who moves beyond his/her own thoughts and ideas and takes action. 'I give up' is not in the finisher's vocabulary. They know that a stumble is not fatal. It's just another opportunity to get back up and succeed. Finishers may fall, but they get back up and continue, determined to cross the finish line."[10]

When the apostle Paul was facing the end of his life, he wrote two very personal letters to his son in the faith, Timothy. The very end of the second letter gave a brief glimpse of how he felt with eternity staring him in the face. There was no complaining. Paul didn't try to blame others for his condition. NO. He said his desire, above all else, was to finish strong. Second Timothy 4:6-8 was Paul's declaration:

> *For I am already being poured out like a drink offering, and the time for my departure is near. I have fought the good fight, I have finished the race, I have kept the faith. Now there is in store for me the crown of righteousness,*

*which the Lord, the righteous Judge, will award to me
on that day—and not only to me, but also to all who
have longed for his appearing.*

3 Common Traits of a Strong Finisher

1. Determination.

An Olympic runner best illustrates the essence of determination and commitment from Tanzania at the 1968 Olympics in Mexico City. His name is John Stephen Akhware, and he will forever be remembered, not for winning a gold medal, but for his determination to finish what he started.

Journalist Roy Tomizawa shared a brief account of what happened:

> Mamo Wolde had already completed the 42-kilometer marathon in the oxygen-thin air of Mexico City, continuing Ethiopian dominance in the footsteps of Abebe Bikila. Wolde had already received his gold medal, and was likely resting somewhere inside the stadium when a humming murmur turned into joyful cheers on that evening of October 20, 1968. A man was walking into the Estadio Olimpico Universitario, his right leg heavily bandaged. He limped decidedly, the result of falling close to the halfway point in the marathon while jockeying for position. He had dislocated his knee and banged up his shoulder in the collision with the pavement. He got treated, and kept running despite the pain, and the cramps. While 17 in the 54-man field did not complete this most grueling of the long-distance competitions, John Stephen

Akhwari of Tanzania, was determined to finish. When asked why he kept running, Akhwari gave one of the most memorable quotes in sporting history: "My country did not send me 5,000 miles away to start the race. They sent me 5,000 miles to finish it."[11]

As you can see, John Stephen Akhware's determination is a perfect example of a strong finisher. He was determined to finish what his country had sent him to do. And no amount of pain and suffering was going to hinder him from his goal.

If you want to finish strong—stay determined.

2. Flexibility.

Leaders who finish strong know that plans don't always work out the way they were intended. Making adjustments "on the fly" is often viewed as a failure of preparation, but the truth is unexpected events do occur—even to the most prepared leader.

Elizabeth McDaid writing in the *Leader's Edge* said:

> A flexible leader has the agility and ability to readily respond to changing circumstances and expectations. Flexible leaders change plans as situations change. This results in an ability to remain productive during times of upheaval or transition. They embrace change, are open to new ideas and enjoy working with a wide spectrum of people.[12]

If you want to finish strong—embrace flexibility.

3. Enthusiasm.

The definition of *enthusiasm* has a spiritual root. The word comes from the Greek word "entheos," which means *God within*.

It's easy to understand that the key to living life with enthusiasm is to have a personal relationship with God.

Norman Vincent Peale once remarked that *"there is real magic in enthusiasm. It spells the difference between mediocrity and accomplishment. ...It gives warmth and good feeling to all your personal relationships."*[13]

*Enthusiastic people are easy to recognize. Enthusiastic people demonstrate an eagerness about the task before them, and as former president Harry Truman observed: "I studied the lives of great men and famous women, and I found that the men and women who got to the top were those who did the jobs they had in hand, with everything they had of energy and enthusiasm."[14]

*Enthusiastic people are contagious. Nobody wants to work around a sourpuss. It's a lot more enjoyable to be around people who are excited about what they are doing. If you're going to get the job done, look for passionate and enthusiastic people about the work, not those who feel like everything is drudgery. Bishop Doane had the same idea when he said: *Enthusiasm is the element of success in everything. It is the light that leads, and the strength that lifts men on and up in the great struggles of scientific pursuits and of professional labor. It robs endurance of difficulty, and makes a pleasure of duty.*[15]

*Enthusiastic people are firm believers in what they are doing and not afraid to take on responsibility. If you've ever had the privilege of working with someone enthusiastic about their job, you know how an otherwise boring day can be turned into an exciting experience. No matter what the challenges are and how big the problems seem, they will always find a way to figure things out and move forward.

If you want to finish strong—get enthusiastic about what you are doing.

ONE MORE THOUGHT…

Why is it so crucial to stay shipshape? Well, I hope I've given you some insight on its importance, but in case you missed the point, let me add one more thought. *Keeping your life in tiptop condition, physically, mentally, and emotionally will keep you from losing your edge so close to the finish line.* Our actions must follow up our words, or we'll end up sitting on the dock while the ship sails without us.

It took Noah over one hundred years to build the ark and he was no spring chicken when he started. Noah kept everything shipshape when the circumstances around him were telling him to give up (see Matthew 24:37-39).

I firmly believe that Noah, despite his limitations, was determined to maintain his construction project *trim, tidy, neat, and with everything in its correct place* until the day the heavens opened, and the rain began to pour.

What about you? Have you determined to keep everything shipshape?

ENDNOTES

1. https://brightdrops.com/motivational-quotes-to-help-you-get-in -shape. Accessed, June 10, 2021.

2. https://www.oxfordreference.com/view/10.1093/oi/authority .2011080310050242 Accessed, June 12, 2021.

3. https://trainingmag.com/leadership-lessons-for-stormy-seas/. Accessed June 12, 2021.

4. https://en.wikiquote.org/wiki/Eleanor_Roosevelt, Foreword (January 1960). Accessed June 12, 2021.

5. https://allthatsinteresting.com/karl-wallenda. Accessed June 13, 2021.

6. https://quoteinvestigator.com/2020/02/04/care/. Accessed June 15, 2021.

7. Stacy Reaoch, "Exercise for More of God Five Reasons to Train Your Body," https://www.desiringgod.org/articles/exercise-for-more-of-god. Accessed June 14, 2021.

8. https://www.theguardian.com/books/2014/apr/04/carrie-stephen-king-horror. Accessed June 15, 2021.

9. https://www.amazingfacts.org/news-and-features/inside-report/magazine/id/10687/t/the-power-of-little-things. Accessed June 17, 2021.

10. http://www.thechoicedrivenlife.com/149-five-qualities-of-a-finisher/. Accessed June 17, 2021.

11. https://theolympians.co/2016/05/20/john-akhwari-champions-do-finish-last/ Accessed June 19, 2021.

12. Elizabeth McDaid, "Flexible Leadership," https://www.leadersedge.com/brokerage-ops/flexible-leadership. Accessed June 19, 2021.

13. Norman Vincent Peale as quoted in *Spiritual Literacy: Reading the Sacred in Everyday Life* (1998) by Frederic Brussat and Mary Ann Brussat, https://en.wikiquote.org/wiki/Enthusiasm. Accessed June 19, 2021.

14. https://www.quotesregister.com/i-studied-the-lives-of-great-men-and-famous-women-and-i-found-that-the-men-and-women-who-got-to-the-top-were-those-who-did-the-jobs-they-had-in-hand-with-everything-they-had-of-energy-and-enthusiasm/. Accessed June 19, 2021.

15. Bishop Doane, p. 208. *Dictionary of Burning Words of Brilliant Writers,* (1895), https://en.wikiquote.org/wiki/Enthusiasm. Accessed June 19, 2021.

9

IT STINKS IN HERE!

(Sailing and Shoveling Go Hand in Hand)

One of the true tests of leadership is the ability to recognize a problem before it becomes an emergency.

—ARNOLD GLASGOW[1]

And Noah and his sons and his wife and his sons' wives entered the ark to escape the waters of the flood. Pairs of clean and unclean animals, of birds and of all creatures that move along the ground, male and female, came to Noah and entered the ark, as God had commanded Noah.

—GENESIS 7:7-9

It's an undeniable fact—leadership can be messy. At some point in your journey, there will be messes to clean up—count on it!

Consider Captain Noah.

Although we are not told specific details, I can't help but believe that Noah understood that once the door to the Ark was closed, it was NOT going to be smooth sailing. How could it be a carefree cruise with so many varieties of animals on board? Animals, no matter how small (think rat) or how big (think elephant), or how wild (think monkey), leave messes behind. And, if they are indoors, that means someone will have to hold their nose and clean it up.

I can't find anywhere in Scripture that when it came time to do a job that no one wanted to do, that Noah dropped anchor and said, *"Ok, now hear this: We are not going any further until all of this mess is cleaned up."* Nope—it didn't happen. What did happen was that Noah understood a fundamental principle: If you want to make it to your destination, *you have to sail and shovel at the same time.*

So, in a literal sense, how did Noah handle the "stinky" problem? An article in *Ark Encounter* online magazine offered the following:

> Inevitably when speaking about Noah and his floating menagerie, the subject comes around to how he managed all that...well, manure. Although ongoing research is continually reducing the total number of animals, as determined by "kinds," that Noah would have taken with him, we must admit this still poses a mounding problem.
>
> A few solutions come to mind. Noah could have dumped it overboard. Or he might have composted it to enrich the plants he probably brought with them. Or Noah might have just let it pile up in the bottom

deck (though adding a certain "ambiance" to their year-long voyage).

One low-tech solution rarely mentioned is the "methane digester." All Noah would have needed was a simple airtight container to hold the manure, the proper bacteria, and a way of piping the resulting biogas to places where it could perform useful work—like a heating, cooking, and lighting inside the ship.

A methane digester was a practical solution for a stinky problem, which probably endeared Noah's kin—or at least their noses—to his resourcefulness.[2]

Writing in *Answers Magazine*, John Woodmorappe offered another view on how Noah and his family could have dealt with all of the animal waste:

As much as 12 U.S. tons (11 m. tons) of animal waste may have been produced daily. The key to keeping the enclosures clean was to avoid the need for Noah and his family to do the work. The right systems could also prevent the need to change animal bedding. Noah could have accomplished this in several ways. One possibility would be to allow the waste to accumulate below the animals, much as we see in modern pet shops.

The danger of toxic or explosive manure gases, such as methane, would be alleviated by the constant movement of the Ark, which would have allowed manure gasses to be constantly released. Secondly, methane, which is half the density of air, would quickly find its way out of a small opening such as a window. There is no reason to believe that the levels of these gasses within the Ark would have approached hazardous levels.

The problem of manure odor may, at first thought, seem insurmountable. But we must remember that, throughout most of human history, humans lived together with their farm animals. Barns, separate from human living quarters, are a relatively recent development.

While the voyage of the Ark may not have been comfortable or easy, it was certainly doable, even under such unprecedented circumstances.[3]

Are you getting the point yet?

As leaders, it is imperative to learn how to do what Noah did without becoming overwhelmed with the smell! I'm not talking about literal manure—but facing the fact that when leading an organization, there will be times when you have to face a pile of problematic issues that, if left unattended, would cause a major stink.

Author Cherry Johnson gave an interesting insight into Noah's challenge while tending to the different kinds of animals,

> Noah was not on the ark with just puppies and kittens. He also shared the boat with ants and fleas, and redbugs. No doubt, some of his passengers became irritating or "got under his skin." Even so, he followed God's instructions and led. Noah understood that regardless of how much you love your organization or how committed

you are, you will encounter problems. The most effective way to handle difficulties is to anticipate them and
lead through them.[4] PROACTIVE VS REACTIVE

And, Cherry Johnson is correct—a wise leader will always
endeavor to anticipate problems before they become so massive
that the organization will be sunk before it ever reaches dry land!

Noah was not the only Biblical leader who faced enormous
leadership challenges.

- Moses was tasked with leading over two million
  Israelites who did nothing but complain and challenge his leadership at every opportunity (Exodus
  17:1-4). Moses learned that in times of difficulty, he
  (and us) must depend on God's wisdom to lead him
  through the difficulties. "Then Moses cried out to
  the Lord."

- David was very young when he discovered that
  leadership is more than playing his instruments
  and singing psalms to the Lord. His training as
  a shepherd (killing a lion and a bear) served him
  well when he faced Goliath. The legacy David left
  behind would not have been possible had he not
  defeated Israel's most dangerous enemy.

- Jesus was no exception when it came to facing leadership challenges. He faced enemies from without
  (the Pharisees and other experts in the law) and
  enemies from within his team, namely Judas. Jesus
  knew that some people would never be satisfied
  with what you do, no matter how you treat them

(Luke 7:29-35). Jesus remained steadfast in His vision and used each challenge as an opportunity to demonstrate God's power.

Whether you are a deliverer of a nation (Moses), or a king clothed with immense power (David), or the Son of God (Jesus), problems, difficulties and challenges will find you—they are a part of the job!

Leadership requires something that lies outside of the orderly world of tools and skills. That something is wrestling with the messiness of the leadership life, where much is unknown and uncontrollable. Succeeding requires taking behavioral risks to create and implement ideas.

—JULIE BENEZET[5]

3 CHALLEGNES THAT ARE A PART OF THE JOB—GET USED TO IT!

Challenge #1. There will be naysayers and scoffers and critics; keep building anyway.

Noah faced challenges from outside his family. No doubt Noah faced tremendous pressure while building something the world had never seen, a gigantic boat. There may not have been a protest outside the construction site, but Noah knew full well that the world was going crazy, and soon God was going to do something about the situation. Noah also knew that he couldn't wait to start building the Ark when heaven opened; by then, it would be too late.

I'm sure the critics were everywhere, but stopping to answer his critics was not something Noah intended to do. All it would have accomplished was to slow the building of the Ark to a crawl. Maybe it's time we take the same approach when the critics attack what we are doing. Remember, those who love you don't need an explanation, and those that hate you won't believe anything you have to say. The best thing to do is "PLOW ON" with your God-given assignment and let the Lord do your fighting for you. After all, every minute you spend answering your critics is another minute you are not working on your assignment.

I've always liked the way Nehemiah approached his critics when they demanded him to stop work on the rebuilding of the wall around Jerusalem:

Nehemiah 6:1-4

When word came to Sanballat, Tobiah, Geshem the Arab and the rest of our enemies that I had rebuilt the wall and not a gap was left in it—though up to that time I had not set the doors in the gates—Sanballat and Geshem sent me this message: "Come, let us meet together in one of the villages on the plain of Ono."

But they were scheming to harm me; so I sent messengers to them with this reply: "I am carrying on a great project and cannot go down. Why should the work stop while I leave it and go down to you?" Four times they sent me the same message, and each time I gave them the same answer.

Nehemiah, [like Noah], placed too much value on the project at hand to be worried about what the critics were saying.

Besides the typical day-to-day challenges of the construction project, Noah could face a potential game-changer. And, what was that? A flood was coming, and it appeared that Noah and his family were the only ones preparing for the impending judgment. Undoubtedly, some people casually walked by the construction site and paid little or no attention to what Noah was doing. They had no idea of the danger that would soon be falling from the sky. I can even imagine some people, after seeing the peril they were in, thinking that if they can't get on the Ark, they might as well try to drag Noah and his family out to drown with them—after all, "If we can't be saved, they shouldn't either!"

> *Criticism is self-hate turned outward. I believe hate is often a sign of weakness, envy and fear. Haters hate on you because you're doing what they cannot, will not or are too afraid to attempt.*
> —JOHN BRUBAKER[6]

I doubt your challenges will hinge on you or your organization building a giant floating box to save humankind. But, the outside obstacles to your success are just as real.

You can count on the fact that there will always be those who will hate your success. It's not that they want to drown you, but bringing you down a peg or two would be just fine. We live in a social media bubble where anyone and everyone can become an army of one, destroying everything in their path. They may lob a grenade of a bad review or fire a missile by posting something negative on Facebook. Whatever the source, when the word-bullets start flying, most organizations (I know anything about) seem to figure out a way to continue the mission.

- Some people will hate you for just being successful, period, no reasons given!
- Some people will feel you don't deserve your success because you didn't take their advice.
- Some people will hate you for daring to go after your dream—while they sit on the couch and watch you rise to the next level.
- Some people will hate you for living a life that is faith-filled while they cower in fear, anxiety, and depression.
- Some people will hate you for shining a light of success that makes their life seem even darker.
- Some people will hate you for deciding to make things happen while they sit back and wonder what happened!

It's like the old saying—there are two ways to build the tallest building in town: Build a taller building, or tear down all the other buildings around it. The majority of people would rather tear you down, so they feel a bit better about themselves, than just step up their game and show up in a more awesome way.

*—**Alexander Heyne**[7]*

Challenge #2. Who Bit Me?

Not only did Noah face challenges from without, he also faced challenges from within. I wonder how long it took Noah to realize that just because the door of the Ark was closed, challenges of a different sort would pop up? Noah and his family had a huge responsibility, namely the care and feeding of a wide variety of animals. No doubt there were times of stress where..."*he probably got bitten and kicked more than a few times.*"[8]

Time and space won't allow me to list all the varieties of animals that might have been the Ark. Suffice it to say that Noah and his family had their work cut out for them.

Out of all of the varieties of animals, there are a few that need to be watched. Some of the critters riding on your Ark may be more of a challenge to your success than a negative Twitter post! Paul Liebman in his article, "Why To Stop Leading People Like Sheep," mentions three animals that might be particularly challenging.

3   Critters You Need to Keep an Eye On

- Tommy the Termite. Think about how alert Noah had to be to watch for critters that munched on wood. Noah knew if you allowed those little devils to go unchecked, he might wake up one day only to realize his big boat was about to sink. Sadly, most of us have met a Tommy Termite at some point—You know, the ones who work undercover to undermine the organization. A wise leader will always be on the lookout for any "holes" caused by Tommy the Termite that might affect the team's performance.

- Donald the Donkey. Have you ever tried to lead a donkey somewhere he didn't want to go? If you haven't, maybe you've watched someone try to convince this stubborn animal to move and stop digging in his heels. It's a challenge to lead others who are so resistant to change they will consciously pull in the opposite direction. If you haven't met Donald the Donkey yet, you will.

- Sally the Sheep. We have all heard how quiet and easy sheep are to lead—right? But the truth is sheep when hungry or provoked will head-butt and bite you. I don't think Noah treated those animals who bite any different than those who didn't. A wise leader will learn to lead those who may bite them even when they (the leader) feel they don't deserve it. Most people (and animals) respond to love, encouragement, and kindness. Phil Liebman observed that...

When as leaders, we treat people like sheep, trying to make them comfortable by guiding them down the path we feel they ought to be on, we actually deprive them of the self-determination and the sense of personal accomplishment that ignites their curiosity and sparks their growth. We stifle them in ways that over time become irreparable.[9]

Challenge #3. Clean-Up on Aisle 5.

Mistakes, mess-ups, and mishaps happen. It's a part of life—sometimes, things go sideways. How many times have we heard that mistakes and failures are just a part of the growth cycle of individuals, who by the way, make up the organization? While the previous question is accurate, we need to learn that if we don't use the mistakes as a "learning experience," all we are doing is walking around with a mop and bucket cleaning up AFTER the mess has been made.

The Bible does not hide that some of the biggest mess-ups happened to some big names you might recognize.

- Noah got drunk.
- Abraham, the man of faith, lied to the king, saying that his wife was his sister.
- Jacob was a liar and schemer.
- Rahab worked as a prostitute.
- Moses, although the great deliverer and lawgiver, committed murder and ran to the desert to hide from his crime.
- King David, a man after God's own heart, messed up when he took another man's wife, and had her husband killed. He then tried to cover it up for over two years.
- Jonah, the prophet, was called by God. Instead of obeying God, he ran the other way and almost caused the death of a shipload of men.
- Simon Peter, who said he would never forsake the Lord Jesus, eventually denied Him three times.

There is a common thread in all of the above. Despite their mess-ups, God still had a plan and purpose for their lives. Just because someone makes a mess does not negate God's plan for their life.

A smart leader will not ignore mess-ups and pretend they never happened. The opposite is that they will acknowledge them and repurpose them as a building block for future success.

You are not helping anyone learn from their mistakes by simply calling for "clean up on aisle 5" without understanding how the mess got there and what to do to avoid it happening again!

> Every day, leadership challenges are going to come for you. From all sides, around every corner, even from within. Leadership—true leadership based on honesty, authenticity and meaningful relationships—takes guts. The kind of leadership that inspires others, serves others, and points them toward a greater purpose and vision...it's hard work. There are many bumps on the path of leadership. Sometimes they're roadblocks. Sometimes the bridge is out entirely. But every challenge is an opportunity. It's a chance to learn about yourself, improve your skills and strengthen the emotional intelligence that's so critical to effective leadership.[10]

Here's the point: There will always be challenges to your leadership (and your organization) from the outside. And, for every challenge you face on the outside there will be ten more challenges from within. There is no use in whining or complaining about it. It is best to be prepared for what kind of challenges you might face and learn how to handle them.

ONE MORE THOUGHT...

Any leader worth their salt will tell you there are times when you have to deal with unpleasant things. Today's leader must learn to "shovel and sail" at the same time. Most leaders I know would rather have a root canal than deal with problems, but the fact remains that challenges will always be a part of the job description—it's a fact of life.

A key point to remember: There will always be people on board your ship (your organization/ministry) who may pose a threat to your leadership. I'm sure Noah could testify that when you have such a large variety of animals, there are bound to be some that won't go along with what you are trying to accomplish (see point #3 above). And, there may come a time when you want to throw the problem overboard. But, by maintaining your integrity, and most of all, your Christian values, you might just be surprised to learn that you can be blessed if you don't give up.

How is that possible?

In Luke 6:22-23, Jesus said,

> *Blessed are you when people hate you, when they exclude you and insult you and reject your name as evil, because of the Son of Man. Rejoice in that day and leap for joy, because great is your reward in heaven. For that is how their ancestors treated the prophets.*

Instead of viewing obstacles as roadblocks, ask God to help you view them as stepping stones to the next level of success. In my life, I have found some of the most difficult "tests" have come right before my biggest blessings. Sadly, many excellent and principled leaders give up too soon and miss out on landing safe and sound on the other side of the flood!

ENDNOTES

1. https://priscillaajacks.wordpress.com/2013/11/21/one-of-the-true-tests-of-leadership-is-the-ability-to-recognize-a-problem-before-it-becomes-an-emergency-arnold-h-glasgow/ accessed August 2, 2021.

2. "Another Meaning to Poop Deck," *Ark Encounter*, August 24, 2012, https://arkencounter.com/blog/2012/08/24/another-meaning-to-poop-deck, accessed August 2, 2021.

3. John Woodmorappe, "Caring for the Animals on the Ark," *Answers Magazine,* March 24, 2009, https://answersingenesis.org/noahs-ark/caring-for-the-animals-on-the-ark/ accessed August 2, 2021.

4. Cherry L.F. Johnson, *In an Ark with the Animals on a Rainy Day,* (New York, NY: YBK Publishers, 2017). p. 39.

5. "The Leadership Life Is Messy: 5 Ideas to Address the Mess," February 18, 2019 Julie Benezet. https://trainingindustry.com/articles/leadership/the-leadership-life-is-messy-5-ideas-to-address-the-mess/ accessed August 5, 2021.

6. John Brubaker, "Why the Most Successful People Have the Most Haters," https://www.entrepreneur.com/article/254282, accessed August 7, 2021.

7. Alexander Heyne, "This is EXACTLY Why People Hate Successful, Healthy, and Happy People," https://modernhealthmonk.com/why-people-will-hate-you-for-being-healthy-and-successful/ accessed August 7, 2021.

8. Cherry L.F. Johnson, *In an Ark with the Animals on a Rainy Day,* (New York, NY: YBK Publishers, 2017). p. 43.

9. Phil Liebman, "Why To Stop Leading People Like Sheep—A Lesson in Human Leadership," https://alpsleadership.com/index.php/2019/10/14/why-to-stop-leading-people-like-sheep-a-lesson-in-human-leadership/ accessed August 17, 2021.

10. InitiativeOne, Leadership Institute, https://www.initiativeone.com/insights/blog/leadership-challenges / accessed August 8, 2021.

10

YOU'RE NEVER TOO OLD TO BUILD YOUR DREAM

(Age Is Just a Number)

I don't believe in age, it's just a number. I believe in energy. Don't let age dictate what you can and cannot do.

—UNKNOWN[1]

Even to your old age and gray hairs
I am he, I am he who will sustain you.
I have made you and I will carry you;
I will sustain you and I will rescue you.

—ISAIAH 46:4

According to Bible scholars, Noah was born in 2928 B.C. He was approximately 480 years old when God instructed him to build the Ark. It wasn't to be any ordinary boat, not by any stretch of the imagination. This boat would be the "lifeboat" of those who would perpetuate the human race, along with a wide variety of animals. Noah could have responded by reminding the Lord how old he was, and what he needed was a rocking chair, not blueprints for a giant floating box. Noah did nothing of the sort.

Noah understood a fundamental principle—*It is not about how many birthdays you've had—it was about the assignment you've been given.*

Fast-forward around 120 years, and Noah has reached the ripe old age of 600 (Genesis 7:11-12). The Ark is ready to sail—the work is complete.

Noah proved that age was NOT a roadblock, and you are never too old to build your dream. Now, before you laugh out loud at that last statement, as if I didn't realize that people today don't exactly live anywhere near 600 years old, I remind you that Noah wasn't looking at the calendar—but the mission he was given. Noah never allowed his age or lack of experience to determine whether he could reach his goal.

On September 8th, 1966, a new television show entitled *Star Trek* aired for the first time. In the beginning, the show didn't garner much attention. Eventually, the show would become one of the most beloved (and copied) television shows of all time. One of the main characters was a Vulcan named Mr. Spock. His famous greeting was *"Live long and prosper."* Even though that phrase was first spoken in the 60s, it still reverberates today. Why? There is something inside us that desires not just longevity of life but a life that impacts those around us. After all, who doesn't want to live a long life and prosper at the same time?

Gauging the impact of someone's life is not just in the length of their days, but in the contribution of their life no matter how long they were on planet Earth.

But, not everyone feels the same way when it comes to aging:

> Given the choice between living 80, 120 and 150 years—or even "forever"—the majority of those polled last month during a talk by popular science journalist, David Ewing Duncan, opted for 80.
>
> Even after being presented with an astonishing array of devices and drugs that could radically extend the average life span, few in the audience changed their votes. When asked why, those who spoke up said it was because they'd rather not prolong the aging process simply for the sake of postponing the inevitable.[2]

Given this aversion to lengthy living, could it be that Mr. Spock was just kidding when he said, *"Live long and prosper"*? Or is it that we have yet to accept the idea that the two concepts can coexist? Even if we haven't been paying attention, there's plenty of evidence to suggest they can.

According to Merriam-Webster.com, the word prosper *means to succeed in an enterprise or activity; especially: to achieve economic success: to become strong and flourishing.*[3]

If where you are today is not where you want to be tomorrow, it's time to change your thinking. The idea is to make the most of what we have, where we are, to do all that we can.

Author and entrepreneur Bob Buford writes:

> None of us knows when we will die. But any one of us, if we wish, may select our own epitaph. Saint

Augustine said that asking yourself the question of your own legacy—"What do I wish to be remembered for?—is the beginning of adulthood."[4]

Thinking about your epitaph when you are young may seem superfluous and out of context with what's going on in your life— "Why think about it now? I have many years before I need to get serious about what I want to be remembered for?" But, my dear friend, death does not discriminate between the old and the young!

The Bible states that life is brief!

> Job 8:9: *For we were born only yesterday and know nothing, and our days on earth are but a shadow.*
>
> Job 9:25: *My days are swifter than a runner; they fly away without a glimpse of joy.*
>
> Psalm 102:11: *My days are like the evening shadow; I wither away like grass.*
>
> James 4:14: *Why, you do not even know what will happen tomorrow. What is your life? You are a mist that appears for a little while and then vanishes.*

Let's be honest about it, "Live long and prosper" is a challenge we all face. For decades, we have lived in a fast-paced microwave society that demands instant gratification. People seldom stop long enough to consider that it is never too late to do something new and different when it comes to their dreams.

To him who knows to prosper
and does it not, to him it is sin.
—**EDWIN LOUIS COLE**[5]

Maybe it is time for a change. Perhaps it's time to do something about your dreams for your future and *stop counting birthdays.* Remember, if you are willing to tolerate your current situation, then your current situation will never change.

If you are ready to make a new start—keep reading.

HERE ARE FOUR THINGS YOU CAN DO—RIGHT NOW!

1. Make A Decision.

One of the most challenging things for some people is to make a decision—about anything. It's one thing to be uncertain about what ice cream you want to order and quite another thing when it comes to your future.

According to Carrie Barron, M.D.:

> Indecision can stem from depression, anxiety, and fear of making the wrong decision, and suffering consequences or remorse. Worry about making a mistake and feeling guilty, remiss, exposed, or ignorant is common. Sometimes, people are paralyzed by a fear of hurting or alienating another.[6]

If you're having difficulty, try asking a few questions:

1. What Do I Want?

Which is a challenge of knowledge. If you don't know what you want, it's impossible to give you the information you need to move to the next level of success.

*Unsuccessful people make decisions based on
their current situation; successful people make
decisions based on where they want to be.*

—ANONYMOUS

2. Am I Willing to Pursue What I Want?

Which is a challenge of motivation. You can take the attitude of "sit and wait" and hope something good will happen, which is what many people do, or you can take the initiative and pursue your dreams with self-motivation that will even astound your closest friends!

*With ordinary talent and extraordinary
perseverance, all things are attainable.*

—THOMAS BUXTON[7]

3. Will I Achieve What I Want?

Which is a problem of persistence. In simple terms, it's called "following through." A life of success is a marathon, not a 110m dash. I have often wondered why people have such trouble when it comes to deciding their future. I've heard all kinds of excuses—and I'm sure you have too.

Things such as...

- I don't have enough money to try something different.
- What if I fail?

- Making a change is not something I am comfortable doing.
- I gave up on my dream years ago—no use in starting now.
- I have been told my dreams are unrealistic.
- I looked at the calendar, and I don't have the energy any longer.
- Age may be just a number, but I have too many numbers!

But, with all the excuses above (and more that I didn't add) there is one factor that keeps many people from realizing that it is never too late to pursue their dreams.

ONE WORD—FEAR!

> Author Les Brown explains it this way: FEAR is the number one obstacle that stops people from achieving their goals. It doesn't matter how talented they are. It doesn't matter how dissatisfied they are with their lives. People continue to trudge along living a life they weren't meant to live because they are afraid.[8]

I have no doubt that Noah and his family faced the fear factor when they entered the Ark. They faced their fears and overcame them because they believed in the promise of God—He would not let them drown, no matter what the circumstances were. And, the Lord will do the same for you if you are willing to fight for what you want and not allow fear to rule your life!

> *Surrendering to fear and allowing*
> *ourselves to be paralyzed by peril isn't*
> *something most of us can afford to do.*
> —BEN CARSON.[9]

2. Be Grateful.

It's possible to become so wrapped up in our daily lives that we forget to express gratitude for what we have. Author Sam Lefkowitz remarked that *"When asked if my cup is half-full or half-empty, my only response is that I am thankful I have a cup."*[10]

Your life may not be what you want it to be, but instead of complaining about what you don't have, start being grateful for what you do have!

Question: What is your attitude toward life—right now? This may come as a shock, but the attitude you have right now is the one you chose. Learning to be grateful doesn't come easy for many people. In fact, for some, it's a lot easier to complain than look at circumstances with a positive attitude.

A positive attitude separates facts from the truth.

The only way someone can make you have a bad attitude is you allow them to control you. The facts may say, "These are my circumstances, and they are bad," but the truth says, "I can overcome them!"

Your attitude will determine your course of action.

Have you ever noticed that the happiest, most positive people don't necessarily have the best of everything? They just make the best of everything. Think about this—does your attitude determine your situation, or does the situation determine your attitude?

Take steps to maintain the right attitude.

Remember—it's a lot easier to maintain the right attitude than to overcome a negative attitude.

Three key questions that will help develop a winning attitude:

1. Am I willing to look inside? To look inside is to determine if my attitude reflects who I am. If it does not measure up, am I willing to pay the price to change or allow tomorrow's problems to kill my attitude today?

2. Am I willing to look around? To look around is to find an accountability partner who will constantly challenge me concerning my attitude. It's essential to associate with the right people because people are like elevators—they will either take you up or take you down!

3. Am I willing to look up? To look up is to realize there is someone greater than myself that I can depend on for daily strength and encouragement. Whether it is prayer, meditation, or just reading a good book of inspirational quotes, find a way to look outside of yourself.

Charles R. Swindoll, in writing about attitude, said:

> The longer I live, the more I realize the impact of attitude on life. Attitude, to me, is more important than

facts. It is more important than the past, the education, the money, than circumstances, than failure, than successes, than what other people think or say or do. It is more important than appearance, giftedness or skill. It will make or break a company...a church...a home. The remarkable thing is we have a choice everyday regarding the attitude we will embrace for that day. We cannot change our past...we cannot change the fact that people will act in a certain way. We cannot change the inevitable. The only thing we can do is play on the one string we have, and that is our attitude. I am convinced that life is 10% what happens to me and 90% of how I react to it. And so it is with you...we are in charge of our Attitudes."[11]

3. Make Your Bed.

In 2014, Admiral William H. McRaven gave a commencement address at the University of Texas. The premise of the speech focused on starting the day right and maintaining an attitude of self-discipline. He grabbed the attention of his young audience by starting his address with this statement; *"If you want to change the world, start off by making your bed!"*

McRaven continued:

> If you make your bed every morning, you will have accomplished the first task of the day. It will give you a small sense of pride, and it will encourage you to do another task and another and another. By the end of the day, that one task completed will have turned into many tasks completed. Making your bed will also reinforce the fact that little things in life matter. If you

can't do the little things right, you will never do the big things right. And, if by chance you have a miserable day, you will come home to a bed that is made—that you made—and a made bed gives you encouragement that tomorrow will be better.

McRaven's address struck a chord with many because of its simplistic but profound message of starting the day right and paying attention to the smallest details.[12]

I think Admiral McRaven would agree that excitement and passion will get you started, but it's self-discipline that will keep you on track. I have discovered in my own life that it is very difficult to experience growth unless there is a measure of self-discipline practiced daily. It's usually not the ones with the most talent or the most skills that end up at the top, but those who have learned the secret of a self-disciplined lifestyle.

> *The common denominator of success lies in forming the habit of doing things that failures don't like to do.*
> —ALBERT GRAY[13]

Five helpful hints for a self-disciplined lifestyle

1. Have clearly defined goals that will keep you on track.

2. Eliminate any distraction that will take you away from your purpose.

3. Pursue your dreams with persistence. A bulldog determination will take you a long way.

4. By maintaining consistency toward your desired end, you will see more accomplishments. It's not easy to do, but a daily routine of consistent habits will pay off in the long run.

5. Self-control is a premium. Even if you fall short, continue to work on self-discipline.

> *You are the same today that you're going to be five years from now, except for two things: The people with whom you associate and the books you read.*
> —**Charles "Tremendous" Jones.**[14]

4. Take Your Mountain.

Do you remember a Bible character named Caleb? He has to be one of my favorites—why? Well, he not only accomplished many great things for the Lord, but maybe his most significant accomplishment came when he was eighty-five years old. Caleb informed Joshua that he wanted the part that was promised to him years before—he wanted his mountain—and he was not too old or afraid to go and take it for himself!

Joshua 14:10-12

> *Now then, just as the Lord promised, he has kept me alive for forty-five years since the time he said this to Moses, while Israel moved about in the wilderness. So here I am today, eighty-five years old! I am still as strong today as the day Moses sent me out; I'm just as vigorous to go out to battle now as I was then. Now give me this hill country that the Lord promised me that day. You*

yourself heard then that the Anakites were there and their cities were large and fortified, but, the Lord helping me, I will drive them out just as he said.

Caleb was not the only "senior citizen" that accomplished great things for the Lord. There is a long list of men and women who trusted the Lord and accomplished great things even in what we would call "advanced years."

When it comes to God's destiny for our lives, there isn't a set time to "call it a day." It will take a lifetime for many people to accomplish everything that God has in store for their lives.

What if some men and women (familiar to us) decided to "retire" and not complete their assignment?

[handwritten: NEVER TO LATE to pursue your dreams]

- The Ark would have never been built (Noah).
- Isaac would have never been born (Abraham and Sarah).
- God's people would have never been delivered (Moses).
- The mountain would have never been captured (Caleb).
- Simeon and Anna would not have seen the coming Messiah.
- Many churches would not have been established by Paul.

ONE MORE THOUGHT...

The question remains—Is it possible to dream big and accomplish goals after what society tells us is our time to "shut it down" and let the younger generation take over? Yes, a thousand times yes. At the age of 58 when most are slowing down, I sped up. Accepting my assignment from the Lord at the invitation of Ron Puryear and the Management Team of World Wide Dream Builders has been the greatest adventure of my life. I believe eternity will reveal that pastoring WWDB's has been one of the most significant contributions of my ministry to the Kingdom of God. Retire? What would a person with purpose retire too? When you're making a difference because you're living your dream, plow on, plow on, plow on until there are no more rows to plow.

For your edification and enjoyment, read the sampling from welbi.com of seniors who accomplished their goals. They did so well beyond what many consider the age when you should be sitting in a rocking chair.

- Minoru Saito from Japan became the oldest person to sail solo and non-stop around the world in 2011 at age 77.
- In 1998, John Glenn became the oldest astronaut when he went to space as part of Space Shuttle mission STS-95 at age 77.
- The oldest person to reach the summit of Mount Everest is Yuichiro Miura who did so at age 80.
- Johanna Quaas, from Germany is recognized as the world's oldest gymnast at age 86.
- Another record-breaker is Fauja Singh, the world's oldest marathon runner. Singh was still participating in marathons as recently as January 2016 when he ran in the Mumbai Marathon at age 104.

- At age 72, Halifax native Hanna Fraser became the 3rd generation of women in her family to achieve a black belt in taekwondo.

- Nola Ochs became the oldest college graduate in 2007 at age 95.

- In 2017, Irish racer Rosemary Smith became the oldest person to drive a Formula 1 car at age 79.

All the seniors on this list deserve respect and admiration. Despite being in their later years, they were able to accomplish extraordinary achievements. People like them prove that anyone can do amazing things at any age.[15]

Have you looked in the mirror and decided that your grey hair (or lack of hair) is God's way of telling you it's time to go sit under a tree and die? I sincerely hope not! Novelist Anne Lamott said,

Sixty, feels exactly like 50, with aching feet and more forgetfulness.... But your inside person doesn't age. Your inside person is soul, is heart, in the eternal now, the ageless, the old, the young, all the ages you've ever been.[16]

GO AHEAD AND DREAM BIG—AND STOP LOOKING AT THE CALENDAR!

ENDNOTES

1. https://thepointofpowerisnow.medium.com/21-september-2021-mind-over-matter-age-is-just-a-number-5785881b5858. Accessed September 10, 2021.

2. "Is There A Cure For Old Age?" https://patch.com/california/watsonville/there-cure-old-age-. Accessed September 10, 2021.

3. https://www.merriam-webster.com/dictionary/prosper. Accessed September 10, 2021.

4. *Bob Buford, Half Time*, (Grand Rapids, MI: Zondervan Publishing, 1994) p. 17-18.

5. Edwin Louis Cole quotes. https://5quotes.info/quote/242496. Accessed September 13, 2021.

6. Carrie Barron M.D., "Why Is It Difficult to Make Decisions?" https://www.psychologytoday.com/us/blog/the-creativity-cure/201408/why-is-it-difficult-make-decisions. Accessed September 13, 2021.

7. Thomas Buxton, 1st Baronet, as quoted in Frank Leslie's Sunday Magazine Vol. XIX (January—June 1886), p. 89. https://en.wikiquote.org/wiki/Perseverance. Accessed September 14, 2021.

8. Les Brown, *Laws of Success,* (Germantown, MD: Lurn Publishing, 2016). p. 34.

9. Ben Carson quotes, https://quotepark.com/quotes/1844649-ben-carson-surrendering-to-fear-and-allowing-ourselves-to-be/ Accessed September 15, 2021.

10. https://www.success.com/john-maxwell-being-well-is-doing-well/ Accessed September 15, 2021.

11. Charles R. Swindoll. https://www.goodreads.com/author/quotes/5139.Charles_R_Swindoll. Accessed September 15, 2021.

12. https://www.nbcnews.com/know-your-value/feature/why-making-your-bed-can-change-your-life-ncna829446. Accessed September 16, 2021.

13. https://jamesclear.com/great-speeches/the-common-denominator-of-success-by-albert-e-n-gray.

14. https://tremendousleadership.com/blogs/tremendous-tracey/five-years-from-now. Accessed September 17, 2021.

15. https://www.welbi.co/blog/10-amazing-accomplishments-by-seniors. Accessed September 17, 2021.

16. http://www.notable-quotes.com/l/lamott_anne.html. Accessed September 17, 2021.

11

FOLLOW ME!

(Exposing Four Fallacies of Followership)

Followership, like leadership, is a role and not a destination.

—Michael McKinney[1]

Follow my example, as I follow the example of Christ.

—1 Corinthians 11:1

Noah was demonstrably a great leader. The Ark, the animals, and his family would have been wiped out without his courage to lead.

Noah is the first man who is said to have been righteous. *"Noah was a righteous man, blameless among the people of his time, and he walked faithfully with God"* (Genesis 6:9). How Noah walked and lived differently is not known, but Noah's life and relationship to God were unique. According to God, Noah was blameless for the darkness that was covering the world.

But, Noah learned to function in another role. He was also a faithful follower. Unlike Adam, Noah followed the Lord's leadership with great trust, and obeyed every instruction.

Noah demonstrated that it is possible to fill both roles—to be a capable leader and a faithful follower.

To complete our assignment, WE TOO must learn to embrace both roles as leaders and followers. General George S. Patton said, *"We herd sheep, we drive cattle, we lead people. Lead me, follow me, or get out of my way."*[2]

God gave Noah the assignment to build the Ark and lead his family and the animals through the flood to dry land. But, at the same time, Noah had to become a faithful follower and trust God to lead and guide him through the most perilous journey of his life.

It's evident from reading the Biblical account that Noah understood how to function in either role. I'm sure there were days on the Ark when like a shepherd, he had to lead, and there were other days when he felt like he was one of the sheep, following the Lord's instructions.

Some days we are the shepherd, and other days we are the sheep!

No matter the title or how many people serve in an organization, we must remember that the Lord has the headship over all principalities and powers.

> *And in Christ you have been brought to fullness. He is the head over every power and authority* (Colossians 2:10).

Jesus Set the Example of Followership

The Son of God...

"modeled the fulfillment of the dual roles of leader and follower and expected the same from His disciples. Though He was a leader in human form on earth, He was a follower of God the Father and carried out God's instructions literally until His death."[3]

His philosophy of being a leader and a follower was summed up when He was accused of breaking Sabbath laws.

Jesus gave them this answer:"Very truly I tell you, the Son can do nothing by himself; he can do only what he sees his Father doing, because whatever the Father does the Son also does. For the Father loves the Son and shows him all he does. Yes, and he will show him even greater works than these, so that you will be amazed" (John 5:19-20).

I find it interesting that when Jesus called His disciples, He never gave them the fine print of what it would mean to follow Him (see author's note[4]). On one occasion, He walked by the seashore and saw two brothers fishing—Peter and Andrew. His invitation was simple; *"'Follow me, and I will make you fishers of men.' Immediately they left their nets and followed him."* (See Matthew 4:18-20).

JESUS

Greek word translated as "follow"…is *akoloutheō*.and It can also mean "accompany" and "assist,"…as well as "follow." We can see that when Jesus was calling people to follow him; he wasn't just saying tag along. Jesus didn't want people to just listen and believe in him from a distance. He was inviting people to come close, to join him, and even help him with his mission. He wanted people to be vitally engaged with him in both learning and doing the work of the gospel.[5]

When Jesus called His first disciples to *follow Him,* He said for them to leave what they are doing to take a new way and walk a different path. They would begin living a life that was totally different from anything they had previously known. Their decision to follow would not only change their lives but would have an impact for all eternity.

How Jesus found and called out all the disciples is not known, but Jesus did say that those who follow Him did not choose Him, but that He chose them.

> *You did not choose me, but I chose you and appointed you so that you might go and bear fruit—fruit that will last—and so that whatever you ask in my name the Father will give you* (John 15:16).

A curious aspect of His calling these men to "follow Him" is they never stopped to ask questions or to inquire what "following" Christ would entail. Maybe they understood what "fishers of men" meant, but I sincerely doubt they did. They dropped what they were doing, and without consulting anyone or asking to read a brochure about His ministry, they followed Him. These men, called to follow Christ, would also become the foundational leaders of the early church. Over and over again, you can see these men functioning in the dual role of leaders of men and followers of Christ (read Acts 1-7).

Paul Followed the Example Set by Jesus

Paul's letter to the Church in Corinth twice implored these young believers to "imitate" him as he "imitates" Christ. *"Therefore, I urge to imitate me"* (1 Corinthians 4:16). *"Follow my example, as I follow the example of Christ"* (1 Corinthians 11:1).

What was Paul saying by inviting young Christians to follow him? Was Paul acting out of arrogance or self-importance by making those statements? Not at all. The last thing Paul wanted to do was to adopt the attitude of "do as I say, not as I do" approach to his responsibility as a leader. Paul knew that his words might be taken out of context. But in the end, his confidence was in the Lord and not in the opinions of men.

The word for imitate, or follower, used by Paul, literally means to mimic. Paul expressed the same attitude in Philippians 3:17. *"Join together in following my example, brothers and sisters, and just as you have us as a model, keep your eyes on those who live as we do."* Have you ever seen little children dress up like their mother or father? Little children learn early on to imitate the example set by their parents, good or bad. Paul is saying that he wanted to live and lead in such a fashion that God's glory and the image of Christ could be seen through him for the benefit of others.

How could Paul say follow me, as I follow Christ? Author Bryan Catherman, writing in the *Salty Believer*, offered some insight:

> When Paul is saying follow me, he is really saying follow Jesus. Only as Paul is filled with the Spirit and sanctified more and more, he is able to demonstrate how Christ lived and instructed us to live. "But why wouldn't Paul have simply instructed people to follow Jesus?" we may still ask. "Why wouldn't Paul have encouraged them to ask, 'What would Jesus do?'" Well, at the time Paul didn't have the Gospels or the New Testament to turn to. As an Apostle, one of his

responsibilities was to model the gospel and write God's revelation under the authority and guidance of the Holy Spirit for future generations. However, I believe he would have said the exact same thing even if he had the 27 books of the New Testament we have today. Paul served as an under-shepherd of Christ and was filled by Jesus himself. The more Paul was full of Jesus the less room he had for himself. As Paul was crucified, daily, he was becoming less. And the more he could be a living example of Christ (even if he could have handed someone God's written Word), the more people could see and experience the Living God through Paul.[6]

The apostle Paul nailed his testimony down when he penned Galatians 2:20: *"I have been crucified with Christ and I no longer live, but Christ lives in me. The life I now live in the body, I live by faith in the Son of God, who loved me and gave himself for me."*

Paul was not shy, nor was he afraid to encourage others to look at his life and follow his example. For me, what made Paul worth following was simply whom he was following. I want to know that the person I'm following is someone I can trust to lead me down the right paths in life. Not paths that lead to destruction of my life, marriage, relationships and dreams.

EXPOSING FOUR FALLACIES OF FOLLOWERSHIP

Followership has taken a bad rap. There is so much misunderstanding about what it means to cultivate the attitude of a follower that it would be impossible to list them all here.

Below are four fallacies that seem to highlight where some have missed the boat completely. SUM TO HAVE
CUMMENTES

1. Following instructions is not essential.

Can you imagine the chaos that would have ensued if Noah decided NOT to follow the Lord's instructions? What if Noah had said, *"I don't need anyone telling me how to build the Ark. I can do this job all by myself."* Thank the Lord Noah didn't take that approach, or we would all be sunk! No, a capable leader understands the importance of not only leading but also following instructions.

> *Folks who follow instructions show that they are cooperative, intelligent, and dependable, while those who disregard instructions can cause obstacles—and safety concerns—down the line.*
> —DAVID NAAR[7]

The Lone Ranger approach to leadership is far past its time. A wise and thoughtful leader will understand that following instructions is just as important as giving instructions to those under their leadership. When we become more important and above the fray that we don't have to listen, learn, or follow anyone, we are more self-absorbed than God ever intended.

2. Following is not as important as leading.

Let's face it—everyone aspires to some leadership position. If that weren't the case, why are leadership conferences, seminars, and webinars overflowing? Just mention the "Leadership Van" is parked outside, and everyone wants to buy a ticket and take a ride. But, on the other hand, when was the last time you saw a sold-out conference on "How to become a great follower?" Wearing the label of a follower doesn't fit nicely on a resume or cause one to brag to fellow organization members.

Author Douglas Smith made an observation about following:

> Following suffers from a serious image problem. Few children aspire to grow up to become followers. Following is not included in selection criteria for colleges, professional schools, scholarships, or awards. In fact, at school, in books and newspapers, in the movies, and on television, following is often condemned as a mindless denial of basic humanity. We are treated to a steady diet of groupies, cult members, and brainwashed masses and are bluntly warned against the horror and destitution of following.[8]

Unfortunately, this fallacy that "following is not as important as leading" has led to many unintended consequences, namely the separation of roles. The truth is that leaders can and should function in both roles, simultaneously, as followers and leaders; for any leader to deny that basic fact is to stand in danger of leading the organization off a cliff.

3. Men lead; women follow.

The question, "Should women be in leadership positions?" is often called the third rail of organizational politics, including the church. The issue of roles between men and women has become a highly charged debate. It's the old idea that women must stay in the background while men lead the way. The issue of gender roles won't be settled any time soon, and it won't be settled here either.

But I would like to point out that history (both church and secular history) has given us remarkable examples of strong, powerful women who led with courage, integrity, and sacrifice.

Sandra Day O'Connor, former Supreme Court Justice, spoke for an entire generation of women when she said:

> For both men and women, the first step in getting power is to become visible to others—and then to put on an impressive show. The acquisition of power requires that one aspire to power, that one believes power is possible. As women that achieve power and exercise it well, the barriers fall. That's why I'm optimistic. As society sees what women can do, as women see what women can do, there will be even more women out there doing things—and we'll all be better off for it. Certainly, today women should be optimistically encouraged to exercise their power and their leadership skills wherever it might take them.[9]

4. Followers are second-class citizens.

When followers are viewed merely as enablers, who push the main leader toward some grand accomplishment, you widen the gap between leaders and followers. Leaders make more money, enjoy more benefits, and even garner the most attention in most cases. While the leader is standing to the crowd's applause, the followers are expected to tag along for the ride (while doing most of the heavy lifting) without the recognition they deserve.

Chuck Violand, writing in *Strategies for Success,* said:

> I think it's time to build a case for followership. After all, following is a critical component of being an

effective leader. Effective leaders provide their followers with opportunities to develop their own leadership skills. In order to do this, leaders must learn both when and how to exercise the following part of leading and the leading part of following.[10]

If leaders were more focused on servanthood and less on "who gets the credit," the role of following would take on a new meaning. One way to start that transformation is to give authority commensurate with the responsibility. Many volunteers (followers) feel they are sometimes responsible for carrying out a task without the authority to make things happen. Conversely, leaders who hold the authority without accepting the responsibility are endangering the team's *esprit de corps*.

Barbara Kellerman said, *"Followers are more important to leaders than leaders are to followers."*[11] I think Kellerman may have a point!

On October 24, 1944, Aubrey S. Newman led a regiment of the 24th Infantry Division as it landed on Leyte Island. Newman took part in General Douglas MacArthur's promise to return in order to retake the Philippines from the Japanese. When the amphibious assault bogged down, Newman rallied his men with a shout that would later become a rallying cry plastered on recruiting posters on every building in the United States. The now-famous battle cry that inspired his men was a simple charge: *"Get the hell off the beach....Follow me!"* The Army would later paraphrase his words on a poster that read: *"Get up and get moving! Follow me!"*

Newman understood the importance of setting the example by leading his men from the front. But he also knew without those same men who were willing to follow him, he would be leading a charge against a fortified enemy by himself.

> *Followers and leaders both orbit around the purpose; followers do not orbit around the leader.*
> —IRA CHALEF[12]

We must never forget that our success is often the result of our ability and willingness to forsake our agenda and follow those who lead us. We have a roadmap that points the way to an abundant and successful life—it's called the Bible.

I have examined some of the fallacies of followership, but let me suggest *10 Rules of the Road for Followers* taken directly from God's Word.

10 RULES OF THE ROAD FOR FOLLOWERS

1. Be careful when you openly challenge your leader.

Numbers 12:1-2: *Miriam and Aaron began to talk against Moses because of his Cushite wife, for he had married a Cushite. "Has the Lord spoken only through Moses?" they asked. "Hasn't he also spoken through us?" And the Lord heard this.*

Questioning a person is completely different than asking that person a question. One is making an accusation, the other is asking for information. Be respectful in the way you approach your leader. It's a matter of the intent and attitude of your heart.

2. *Always keep your hearts open for the wisdom shared by your leaders.*

> Proverbs 19:20-21: *Listen to advice and accept discipline, and at the end you will be counted among the wise. Many are the plans in a person's heart, but it is the Lord's purpose that prevails.*

You choose to follow someone because of your belief in their credibility. So, listen, learn and grow.

3. *Be known as a hard worker.*

> First Thessalonians 5:12-13: *Now we ask you, brothers and sisters, to acknowledge those who work hard among you, who care for you in the Lord and who admonish you. Hold them in the highest regard in love because of their work. Live in peace with each other.*

4. *Show respect and follow the example of your leaders.*

> Hebrews 13:7-8: *Remember your leaders, who spoke the word of God to you. Consider the outcome of their way of life and imitate their faith. Jesus Christ is the same yesterday and today and forever.*

5. *Demonstrate a positive attitude.*

> Hebrews 13:17: *Have confidence in your leaders and submit to their authority, because they keep watch over you as those who must give an account. Do this so that their work will be a joy, not a burden, for that would be of no benefit to you.*

6. *Maintain your testimony as a faithful follower of Christ.*

Colossians 3:12: *Therefore, as God's chosen people, holy and dearly loved, clothe yourselves with compassion, kindness, humility, gentleness and patience.*

7. *Pray for your leader.*

First Timothy 2:1-2: *I urge, then, first of all, that petitions, prayers, intercession and thanksgiving be made for all people—for kings and all those in authority, that we may live peaceful and quiet lives in all godliness and holiness.*

8. *Represent your leader well.*

Colossians 4:5: *Be wise in the way you act toward outsiders; make the most of every opportunity.*

9. *Rejoice with those who rejoice.*

First Chronicles 29:10: *David praised the Lord in the presence of the whole assembly, saying, "Praise be to you, Lord, the God of our father Israel, from everlasting to everlasting."*

10. *Follow your leader; but don't turn off your mind.*

Colossians 2:8: *See to it that no one takes you captive through hollow and deceptive philosophy, which depends on human tradition and the elemental spiritual forces of this world rather than on Christ.*

ONE MORE THOUGHT...

If you have been involved in leadership for very long, you know how tough it can be. Leadership on any level requires followers. Instead of asking, "Who's in charge or who's the leader?" we might rephrase the question to ask, "Who is the leader following, and how does one know it?" The questions leaders ask themselves need to change from *skill-based to character-based.*

If we are not careful, our focus will be on the competence and skill of a leader rather on what shapes a leader's life, character, and decision-making process. If a leader is led by another individual, a philosophy, a school of thought, or personal appetites, that ultimately affects the capacity of the leader to bring about transformational change.

Joseph M. Stowell, retired president of Cornerstone University, summed up the issue of *followership* when he penned these words in his book, *Following Christ: Experiencing Life the Way It Was Meant to Be.*

Dr. Stowell said:

> Following is the mark of the most successful leaders. Yet, when our task of leading is done, we ourselves will still be followers. Leading is a temporary assignment; following is a lifelong calling.[13]

ENDNOTES

1. https://www.leadershipnow.com/followershipquotes.html. Accessed September 28, 2021.

2. George S. Patton, As quoted in Pocket Patriot: Quotes from American Heroes (2005) edited by Kelly Nickell, p. 157. https://en.wikiquote.org/wiki/George_S._Patton. Accessed September 29, 2021.

3. Cherry L.F. Johnson, *In an Ark with the Animals on a Rainy Day,* (New York, NY: YBK Publishers, 2017). p. 97.

4. Author's Note: For an in-depth look at what it meant for these disciples to follow Christ I encourage the reader to study Matthew chapter 10, with emphasis on verses 16-19. These disciples were charged with a mission to carry the Gospel, but they were also warned about the cost. They had to learn the dual role of leaders and followers in the heat of the battle.

5. "A quick look at the Greek word for 'follow,'" https://margmowczko.com/a-look-at-the-word-follow-akoloutheo/ Accessed September 29, 2021.

6. Bryan Catherman, "Follow Me as I Follow Christ?" https://www.saltybeliever.com/blog/ltybeliever.com/2014/02/follow-me-as-i-follow-christ.html. Accessed October 1, 2021.

7. David Naar, "What Is the Importance of Following Instructions?" https://www.reference.com/world-view/importance-following-instructions-40833e83f4c0a422. Accessed October 1, 2021.

8. Douglas K. Smith, *The Following Part of Leading,* ed. Frances Hesselbein, Marshall Goldsmith, and Richard Beckhard (San Francisco: Jossey-Bass, 1996), 202.

9. Sandra Day O'Connor, "The Majesty of the Law: Reflections of a Supreme Court Justice" April 2004. https://www.thecut.com/2018/03/25-famous-female-leaders-on-empowerment.html. Accessed October 2, 2021.

10. Chuck Violand, "Strategies for Success," https://sfs.jondon.com/13093/blog/dont-disrespect-followership-part-1. Accessed October 3, 2021.

11. https://www.leadershipnow.com/followershipquotes.html. Accessed October 3, 2021.

12. Ira Chalef, https://www.leadershipnow.com/followershipquotes.htm. Accessed October 5, 2021.

13. Joseph M. Stowell, *Following Christ: Experiencing Life the Way It Was Meant to Be.* (Grand Rapids, MI. Zondervan, 1996). p. 40.

12

ALWAYS LOOK FOR THE RAINBOW, AFTER THE STORM
(The Promise of Better Days Ahead)

My heart leaps up when I behold
A rainbow in the sky:
So was it then my life began;
And learned it's time to fly.
—WILLIAM WORDSWORTH (1770-1850)[1]

And God said, "This is the sign of the covenant I am making between me and you and every living creature with you, a covenant for all generations to come: I have set my rainbow in the clouds, and it will be the sign of the covenant between me and the earth."
—GENESIS 9:12-13

The story of Noah and the Ark is one of the most dramatic and talked-about stories in the entire Bible.

The story of the flood has been told and retold countless times. If you've ever attended Sunday School, you heard how Noah and his family saved the animals from destruction and how God promised He would never destroy the earth again with a flood.

Just a brief refresher:

- There was a world filled with sin and violence.
- A holy God unleashed a flood to wipe out His creation.
- Noah's family was chosen by the Lord to represent the entire human race.
- A selection of animals was chosen to be saved.
- Noah was successful because of his obedience to God's command to build something that the world had never seen before—a giant floating box.
- Eventually, the rain ceased, and the waters receded.
- Noah and his family left the boat to start a new life, along with the animals.
- Noah led his family in worship, offering sacrifices, with thanksgiving to God for bringing them through the flood.
- God showed Noah a rainbow and promised never to flood the earth again.
- The rainbow is still visible today—and has a message for Mankind.

Have you ever wondered why God chose a rainbow? After all, an all-powerful God could have chosen any sign or method to convey His willingness to never destroy the population again with a flood.

But, He chose a rainbow.

Author Mark Woods offered some very helpful insight:

> One reason is that there's a sort of poetic appropriateness about it. Rainbows appear after storms as the light from the sun hits the water droplets in the air and breaks into the different colors we don't normally see. A light rain may still be falling, but generally speaking you know when you see the rainbow that, no matter how fierce the storm may have been, it's over. You don't have to worry about rain never stopping.
>
> But the other reason is this. The Hebrew word isn't "rainbow," it's just "bow," as in "bow and arrow." It is a war bow, a deadly weapon. There has been terrible destruction on the earth, and God has done it. He has rained down floods that have exterminated every living thing apart from what's in the ark. We are to imagine him taking aim at the world from heaven. And the point about the bow that he "sets in the clouds" is that it's pointing the wrong way. It cannot be used as a weapon to threaten the world anymore.[2]

When you see a rainbow, it has at least two messages:

First, There Will Be Better Days Ahead.

The rainbow had a message not just for Noah, but for all of us. The terrible storm had passed, the danger was over, and it was safe to start over again. So, the same message is conveyed to us; no matter our background, religious affiliation, skin color, or economic standing, we can trust God, even in the most difficult of circumstances.

I am not saying there will always be the outcome we want. I am not saying that we will never face challenges even after the storm has passed. NO. I am NOT suggesting that at all. I am saying that God has promised that He will walk with us—in the storm—and He will walk with us after the storm has left unspeakable damage. He is not a Heavenly Father who abandons His children in tough times.

No matter where you are in life, horrific storms have a way of finding you. I've discovered that most Christians are either in a storm now or just came through one—it seems to be an ongoing cycle.

But, we can take heart—we have many promises from Scripture that God will not leave us without His care and protection even when the "Mother of all storms" tries to overwhelm us.

Below is a sample of His many promises that have been a wonderful resource to me in times of trouble.

Isaiah 43:2

When you pass through the waters,
I will be with you;
and when you pass through the rivers,
they will not sweep over you.
When you walk through the fire,
you will not be burned;
the flames will not set you ablaze.

Isaiah 66:9

"Do I bring to the moment of birth
and not give delivery?" says the Lord.
"Do I close up the womb
when I bring to delivery?" says your God.

Psalm 62:1-2

Truly my soul finds rest in God;
my salvation comes from him.
Truly he is my rock and my salvation;
he is my fortress; I will never be shaken.

Jeremiah 29:11

"For I know the plans I have for you," declares
the Lord, "plans to prosper you and not to harm
you, plans to give you hope and a future."

I'm not asking you to look for a rainbow with a leprechaun holding a pot of gold. That's a fantasy. For me to ask you to look for a rainbow is a metaphor—it's a way of saying, "Don't give up, there are better days ahead." Difficult days may seem to last forever, but the rainbow is a reminder that "This too shall pass—it didn't come to stay!"

When we are going through the storm, it can be hard to cling to all of the promises we've learned throughout the good days. But often the storm is used to compound what we learned when everything was going just right. The truth is we need the storms. As uncomfortable and painful as these seasons are in life, they grow us and stretch us.[3]

Stop Complaining and Start Thanking!

Trying to stay positive in the middle of a flood isn't something most of us are good at—or accustomed to. If we are honest, we have to admit we are NOT very optimistic by nature. Just the opposite—by nature, we're complainers. Have you noticed that it is a lot easier to complain than to offer praise and thanksgiving when our circumstances turn sour? When our children were growing up, I don't remember when we had to sit them down and teach them how to complain. They just figured it out all by themselves.

It seems our entire nation is infected with a virus—no, not the one you're thinking about—it's a virus of COMPLAINING. We complain about everything—and it's getting worse with each passing day.

HAVE A PLAN & PLAN TO WORK

> Nothing is easier than fault-finding. No talent, no self-denial, no brains, no character, is required to set up in the grumbling business. But those that are moved by a genuine desire to do good have little time for murmuring or complaint.
>
> —ROBERT WEST[4]

Noah never complained about his situation. Think of all the preparations Noah had to make—and, he never complained—not once. And if he did, his grumbling didn't warrant a mention in the Scripture. It's past time to stop complaining about what we don't have and start being thankful to God for what we do have! Billie Kaye asked me a question years ago. She asked, "What if we woke up tomorrow morning with only the things we were thankful for today?" I immediately thought of family, friends, health, ministry and all the blessings of life. We take so many things in life for granted. Great question, think about it.

Consider what Noah DIDN'T complain about:

- That God chose him to build an Ark.
- That there were days when he had to stop work and find enough food to take care of the animals.
- That his neighbors were going to think he was crazy for such an insane attempt to build something the world had never seen.
- That he was too old (around 600 years) to attempt such an undertaking.
- That once inside the Ark, he had to learn to sail and shovel at the same time.
- That God chose him to start over with just his family and some animals.

Instead of griping and complaining about the challenges he faced, Noah offered praise and thanksgiving to the Lord. He was thankful to God for keeping him and his family (and the animals) safe and secure during the flood. *"Then Noah built an altar to the Lord and, taking some of all the clean animals and clean birds, he sacrificed burnt offerings on it"* (Genesis 8:20).

The challenge for us is to remember to be thankful even when we are faced with difficulties. Our flood may not be of the physical type (like Noah), but we all have difficulties that may overwhelm us.

As leaders, we need to learn how to face them positively when facing daily challenges. Whether we like it or not, those in our organization look to us to provide a "north star" of hope when the flood of difficulties starts to rise. No organization is exempt from problems and challenges, but the successful ones will face them head-on and not allow negativity and complaining to rule the day.

I pray that we will never be so consumed with the daily grind that we become too proud or complacent to turn to the ONE who can infuse joy back into our business, home, or church.

May I remind you that the Bible has much to say on the subject of praise and thankfulness?

For instance:

Ezra 3:11

With praise and thanksgiving, they sang to the Lord:
"He is good; his love toward Israel endures forever."
And all the people gave a great shout of
praise to the Lord, because the foundation
of the house of the Lord was laid.

Psalm 7:17

I will give thanks to the Lord because of
his righteousness; I will sing the praises
of the name of the Lord Most High.

Psalm 9:1

I will give thanks to you, Lord, with all my
heart; I will tell of all your wonderful deeds.

Philippians 4:6-7

Do not be anxious about anything, but in every
situation, by prayer and petition, with thanksgiving,
present your requests to God. And the peace of God,
which transcends all understanding, will guard
your hearts and your minds in Christ Jesus.

Perhaps the most beloved psalm on the subject of praise and thanksgiving is Psalm 100. This psalm has been viewed as the "crème de la crème" of Old Testament praise hymns. Packed into a few verses, it contains everything we want or expect when praising and extolling the goodness and mercy of God.

Psalm 100:1-5

Shout for joy to the Lord, all the earth.
Worship the Lord with gladness;
come before him with joyful songs.
Know that the Lord is God.
It is he who made us, and we are his;
we are his people, the sheep of his pasture.
Enter his gates with thanksgiving
and his courts with praise;
give thanks to him and praise his name.
For the Lord is good and his love endures forever;
his faithfulness continues through all generations.

Praise is a choice, an act of our will. We should never take for granted the privilege we have when entering into God's presence.

Just because He has invited us in does not mean we should treat Him with disrespect or a carefree attitude.

We approach Him with a *"Shout for joy."* This phrase means to "blast with a trumpet." Those who think the church is supposed to be a place of hushed whispers are challenged by this statement. When we come into His presence, the Lord is saying we should announce our arrival with a gleeful exclamation of praise, not barge in like a herd of buffalo!

Three Lessons We Can Learn about Praise from Psalm 100

1. *When we praise Him, we can know others better.*

"Shout for joy to the Lord, all the earth." You notice the psalmist did not say, "Shout for joy to the Lord, all of Israel." Instead, he said, "all the earth." The joyful shout of praise is not confined to one group or class of people. People of all races, places, and backgrounds are included. Praise is a universal language and favors no person. It doesn't matter where you are or what country you live in; praise can break down walls and remove obstacles.

> *After this I looked, and there before me was a great multitude that no one could count, from every nation, tribe, people and language, standing before the throne and before the Lamb. They were wearing white robes and were holding palm branches in their hands. And they cried out in a loud voice: "Salvation belongs to our God, who sits on the throne, and to the Lamb"* (Revelation 7:9-10).

2. *When we praise Him, we will do our work better.*

"Worship the Lord with gladness; come before him with joyful songs." The word for *"gladness"* is the word for "mirth." Serving the Lord is not supposed to be hard or boring. There are times when a Sunday morning service looks more like a funeral than a celebration. Serving the Lord is something we get to do, not something we have to do.

3. *When we praise Him, we will know ourselves better.*

Here is what I know about myself: I am not God, and I'm glad! It is God who made each of us unique and special. That means we have a purpose and destiny, and He has promised to lead and guide if we will only let Him. Sheep need a shepherd to protect and guide them to the "still waters" and "green pastures" (see Psalm 23).[5]

Second, a Rainbow Also Speaks of God's Grace to All Mankind!

Not only does the rainbow speak of a promise of better days ahead, but it is also a reminder of God's unspeakable grace toward a sinful world. Just as the Ark was a physical vehicle to save Noah and his family, God has provided salvation from sin and death as demonstrated by Christ on the cross. God's grace is available to anyone who will receive Christ's payment for their sin. When you receive Christ, He becomes your "Ark of safety" for your soul!

Grace is God's best idea. His decision to ravage a people by love, to rescue passionately, and to restore justly—what rivals it? Of all his wondrous works, grace, in my estimation, is the magnum opus.
—MAX LUCADO[6]

The next time you look in the distance and see a rainbow, remember that it speaks of a promise...that you will never go beyond God's reach...that's hope—and that's grace!

Let the following words of Scripture burn in your heart.

Ephesians 2:4-5

But because of his great love for us, God, who is rich in mercy, made us alive with Christ even when we were dead in transgressions— it is by grace you have been saved.

Psalm 103:8

The Lord is compassionate and gracious, slow to anger, abounding in love.

Titus 2:11-12

For the grace of God has appeared that offers salvation to all people. It teaches us to say "No" to ungodliness and worldly passions, and to live self-controlled, upright and godly lives in this present age.

2 Timothy 1:9

He has saved us and called us to a holy life—not because of anything we have done but because of his own purpose and grace. This grace was given us in Christ Jesus before the beginning of time

ONE MORE THOUGHT...

Noah and his family endured a year of rain, rising floodwaters mixed with uncertainty about the future. No doubt Noah communicated to his family the promise that God gave him, but the idea of floating helplessly above a catastrophic flood must have created days of uncertainty. Noah and his family only had God's promise to survive—but, that's all they needed!

One of the most difficult challenges is to look for a rainbow in the midst of pain and difficulty. I'm sure there have been days when you thought that the flood of problems would take you under, only to realize the promises of God would keep you afloat.

One of my favorite hymns is "O Love That Wilt Not Let Me Go," written by Scottish minister George Matheson. You may have sung the hymn in church without knowing it was birthed out of his pain.

By the time Matheson was twenty, he was almost completely blind. According to Matheson, *"I was at that time alone...Something had happened to me, which was known only to myself, and which caused me the most severe mental suffering. The hymn was the fruit of that suffering."*[7] The third verse speaks directly to his pain and declares that he will do something that we need to learn.

"I will," he said,

"Trace the rainbow through the rain."
O Joy that seekest me through pain,
I cannot close my heart to thee;
I trace the rainbow through the rain
And feel the promise is not vain
That morn shall tearless be.[8]

ENDNOTES

1. William Wordsworth (1770-1850), "My Heart Leaps Up," https://poets.org/poem/my-heart-leaps. Accessed October, 15, 2021.

2. "Noah's Ark: After the storm, why did God use a rainbow as a sign?" https://www.christiantoday.com/article/noahs.ark.after.the.storm.why.did.god.use.a.rainbow.as.a.sign/80967.htm. Accessed October, 16, 2021.

3. https://rosevinecottagegirls.com/god-in-the-storm-trusting-god/ Accessed October, 16, 2021.

4. Robert West, reported in Josiah Hotchkiss Gilbert, *Dictionary of Burning Words of Brilliant Writers* (1895), p. 420. https://en.wikiquote.org/wiki/Complaints. Accessed October, 16, 2021.

5. Author's Note: The section "Three Lessons We Can Learn About Praise from Psalm 100" was excerpted from my previous book, *Growing in Favor—Daily Devotions for Walking in Blessing,* (Shippensburg, PA: Destiny Image Pub., 2018) p. 258. This devotional, along with other resources may be ordered directly from our website @ https://www.plowon.org.

6. Max Lucado, God's Grace Quotes, https://www.wow4u.com/godsgracequotes/ Accessed October, 17, 2021.

7. https://flpc.org/o-love-that-wilt-not-let-me-go-2/ Accessed October, 20, 2021.

8. https://www.hymnal.net/en/hymn/h/432. Accessed October, 20, 2021.

13

DREAMING WITH THE DIAMONDS

I've been in business for myself for over 40 years. I've talked with successful people around the world for almost that long.

And I have personally never known anyone who's become extremely successful or done anything great without being a dreamer. You have to have a dream, you have to have a work ethic, and you have to choose to have a great attitude with people.

The truth is, I don't believe you will have a great work habit or have a great attitude with people if you don't have a great dream.

The dream is what pulls you, what motivates you, and what empowers you to become successful in order to do great things to glorify God. I believe with all my heart that one of the greatest gifts the good Lord has ever given us is the ability to dream.

BRAD DUNCAN

One of the truly great gifts God has given each of us at birth is the power to dream. Also, within each of us is the ability to make that dream a reality and ultimately, what we do with that dream is our gift back to God. There is example after example of individuals who chose to make it happen, those who watched it happen, and those who did nothing and simply wondered what happened. When you believe in your dream, you think about it every day, you enthusiastically talk about it, and you treat it as a matter of life or death. Ultimately, when you consistently act upon it each and every day, doors will open and people will come into your life to help you achieve those dreams.

Dream big,

GLEN BAKER

I believe God created in each of us the natural instinct to dream and to have goals and desires. He also gave us the ability and ambition to go after those goals and dreams. Dreams have always been our motivations—not our motives. They get us out of our comfort zone. I believe God even taught us how to dream when He said, "In my house are many mansions." God even talked about the streets of heaven being gold and heaven shining like a glorious stone.

It has never been about "the things." It's been about the life those things would allow us to live. People often say to a dreamer, "All you think about is money." But in reality, what they don't understand is that we wanted to take care of all the things that cost money so that we didn't have to constantly think and worry about "money."

As a wife, mom, daughter, and friend, my dreams have always been about wanting the best for my family and friends. To be able to take care of my parents and show them how grateful we are for them. To raise our children the way we thought was best, not just what we could afford. I wanted to become so financially stable that God could use everything we have to be a blessing to others. What a dream!

JOYA BAKER

The year was 1989. I remember entering a room filled with people that had what Noah had. A dream. At that meeting, I heard the speaker say, "Get a dream so big it includes others." Many other leaders helped me to understand the power of the dream. It drove me when I was excited and helped me to continue on when times got tough.

MATT TSURUDA

I was taught that "a dream is the seed of a vision." A dream is a starting place. The name of our organization is World Wide Dream Builders for a reason. We don't give dreams; we find dreamers and then help them build that dream into a vision that will motivate them to build that vision. A dream is necessary, like breathing is necessary. If you stop breathing, your body will die and you cannot work. If you stop dreaming, your vision will die and you will not work. You will just spend your life seeking pleasure to fill the void in your soul until your body finally stops breathing.

JIM PURYEAR

A productive dream is not a fantasy. It is something that can actually be accomplished with the right tools, mentors, and effort. The missing key for most people is that the fulfillment of any worthwhile dream always has a price.

The real question is, will we pay the price to discipline our-selves in the short term for rewards in the long term? We all want to live like the top 1%, but what are we doing daily that the other 99% are not doing? Will we sacrifice short-term pleasure for long-term prosperity?

No matter what we choose, we will feel pain; it is either the pain of discipline or the pain of regret.

GREG DUNCAN

Dreaming is the unlimited ability to imagine anything, anywhere, anyone that we want in our lives. It is the intangible world that inspires us to turn our desires into reality. It would be a shame to waste this God-given gift, so never stop dreaming.

DAN and SANDY YUEN

Question: What is the difference between your "dreams" and your "wishes"? There is much confusion around these two words. The answer is that dreams are backed by a commitment and consistent effort; wishes are not. This is why we love Paul's book. The dream is the spark that starts the fire within you. The dream is the catalyst that gets you started and moving down the road. The dream is what sustains you and motivates you to overcome whatever challenges stand in your way. Simply stated, people who give up do not have a strong enough dream to sustain them through the tough times. Everyone wishes they could achieve great things, but your dream is the essential fuel that sustains you on the road to accomplishment. Without a dream, there is no doer!

BILL and SANDY HAWKINS

The *power of a dream* is one of the greatest things given to mankind. It gives us the ability to envision our future, to make the decisions to adjust our choices on a daily basis, and to make that future a reality.

We believe all of us were created to prosper, and we have seen that so many times throughout our own life. When we are not focused on accomplishing the dreams God gave us, we are not living our life to the fullest. Dreams breathe life into everything we do.

RYDER and NICOLE ERICKSON

Personally and as a couple we have seen the power of a dream in our life. Every time we have not had a dream in front of us, we have found ourselves slipping into complacency, a critical spirit, and a lack of gratitude. A dream to us is so much more than just an accomplishment or a milestone. A dream to us is a CONSTANT pursuit of improving ourselves. Not settling. And most importantly, not making our lives just about us, but about serving others and helping them accomplish a life of meaning and purpose. It is about running toward the things in life that add value and are lasting. It's about showing others who have lost hope, been mistreated, or have never been loved or believed in, that there is so much value in their life! And that their life is worth every moment.

RYAN and NOELLA OLYNYK

One of my great heroes in life once said, "A dream is a compelling awareness of what could or should be in your life, accompanied by a growing sense of responsibility to do something about it." Meaning that a dream cannot only be something that you merely wish for. It must be something that you not only think about, enthusiastically talk about, and vividly imagine—you must desire it with all your heart.

When it goes from your head to your heart, you will do whatever it takes to bring that vision for your life into fruition. The responsibility you feel to take action toward your dreams is, in my opinion, the greatest differentiator between a dream, and a vague request.

Your actions tell the story about how bad you truly want it.

We live in a culture of talkers, walkers, and balkers. These are people who are trying to close the gap between their dreams and their reality with their words instead of their behavior.

There is a dream God has placed in your heart because of the purpose for your life. And as we pursue purpose, our dreams follow us.

Your friend,

TREVOR BAKER

A dream must move you into action. It must be something you cannot live without. My most significant dreams of accomplishment made me laugh, cry, and feel hugged, loved, and inspired. There were people in my life that God blessed and honored me with. They were family, friends, and amazing relationships who maybe for a season but never without a reason, blessed and empowered me to live out my full potential. Figure out your passionate dreams and go after them with all of your might. It is worth it!!

LESLIE RICE

You'll only perform in life at the level of expectation that you have for yourself. If you don't dream, you'll never raise the expectation for your life. So, it all begins with a dream. The dream is the seed, the beginning. A receptive mind can receive a dream, but a committed mind can sustain a dream. One of the greatest gifts God has given us, outside of salvation, is the ability to dream and the ambition to pursue those dreams.

PETE and RACHAEL HERSHALMAN

We have seen many people struggle to get what they want out of life, not because they can't, but because they don't verbalize and visualize their dreams. There is great power in speaking what you want to achieve and in imagining what you want to become a reality. If you want your dreams to come true, you need to talk about them often, think about them deeply, and wholeheartedly move toward them! Dream BIG—Work Hard—Make It Happen!

DAVID and JAIMEE FELBER

The greatest gift God gave you is the ability to dream, and when you have the right vehicle and you have a major definite purpose, you're unstoppable. The dream gives purpose, it gives you focus, and most importantly, it gives you hope because hope deferred makes the heart grow weary. So never stop pursuing your dreams; it brings joy in the journey.

BOB and SHELLY KUMMER

I've found that dreaming is a muscle that easily atrophies when unused. When you grow up in an environment of scarcity thinking and the dinner-table decree of "don't get your hopes up" mentality, it is all too often a hard habit to change.

I found that you can break free of that bondage with the proper association and the faith that you have been put on this earth for major impact.

I am motivated by the principle: If there is no faith in the future, there's no power in the present. You bring meaning to your life when there is power in today!

TRACEY EATON

Dream big, find a worthy cause bigger than yourself, and find an association/community that promotes your journey. Stay strong in whatever life brings you. Declare your vision and where you are going every morning. Post reminders everywhere you turn and your belief will take you on a great adventure toward your dream.

La figlia di un re,

Kimberly Eaton

We correlate a dream with a vision. To have a vision is to believe that something wonderful can happen in your future. We believe writing things down is one step to accomplishing your dreams. We wrote down our children's names when we got engaged in 1996: Isaiah, Gabriel and Elisha-Joy. We dreamt of having 2 boys and a girl. Isaiah was born first in 1999, then Gabe in 2000, and Elisha-Joy in 2004.

The life we have was a dream that was created by the powerful association with the other leaders and Diamonds in the business. We saw what was possible.

Write it down, dream big, and get around other dreamers!

Howie and Theresa Danzik

Growing up there was no class or encouragement on the importance of a dream. I didn't know that dreams were possible until I saw people who had a desire to pursue one. They enthusiastically talked about where they were going and what they were doing. The vision was so clear for them. I then made a dream board with what seemed like childlike dreams in 2009. Then in 2017 my family and I were able to accomplish every single dream on that board. Our dreams have guided us through the best and toughest of times.

The power of the dream and association is what gives you the strength to accomplish whatever you set your heart's desire on. Rather than say impossible, say "I'm possible."

Mandy Yamamoto

The dream—how important it is that this country has a Name for her: The American Dream. How important then should it be for ALL of her people to have their own personal dream? It's everything.

When I was young, it was so easy to dream. The possibilities were endless, my dreams were already etched in stone. Life was going to be EPIC....dreams of being pretty, smart, popular, fun, accomplished, and successful were right around the corner. Hold on now, not so fast. *Pretty* turned into crooked teeth, hair that never curled, and a body that developed so slowly that my nickname was "the new doll flatsy." *Smart* was never above a B-, difficulty learning, and always feeling hungry and tired in class. *Popular* was the last one to be picked for any team and *happy* turned into sad because I felt like such a loser. *Accomplishment* became an endless grind that was never enough and *success* was hollow, short-lived, difficult to define, and at one point not worth the effort to continue. What had happened to my epic dream? Absolutely nothing, for it was with me the whole time. Teaching me to recognize my true beauty, identifying my gifts outside of a classroom, connecting me to people that appreciated and valued me, finding accomplishments through building something of my own, and striving for significance instead of success. It wasn't always how I imagined, but my dream has afforded me the discipline, grit, and courage to live my best life ever!

Lynn Radford

The Dream drove me to change—and change I needed. Once I witnessed people who were living the dream of freedom and who had the respect and admiration of thousands of other people, I knew I wanted to know them, be with them, and be like them. You cannot put a price tag on true freedom with control of the clock and calendar. I had to fight naysayers, ridicule, and non-believers. The strength and energy to win that battle came from the dream. Now over 30 years and counting.

FRANK RADFORD

I've gotten this question throughout my life, "How did you make it through SEAL training when 85% of your class did not?" When I understood the power of the dream, my answer changed. The power of the dream has served us well in our lifetimes. It was the dream of rebuilding an airplane that I flew in when I was 15 years old that led us to Amway and WWG, which brought us financial independence in our late 20s and early 30s. When you understand the power of the dream, anything is possible!

MIKE and ROBIN CARROLL

I've always said since I was very young that I'd be retired before I was 35 years old. But by the time I was 30 years old, I had no vehicle to get there and couldn't even imagine how I could possibly get there. All I could do was just talk about it.

But in 1980 everything changed. I saw the business and knew in my heart that this was the vehicle that could get us there.

Like most everyone else in the beginning, it was all about money, money, and more money.

And within a few short years, after meeting leaders like Ron Puryear and Bill Britt, we were even more convinced that our dreams could come true. But not only could they come true for us, but we could help thousands of others realize their dreams.

And sure enough, 3 1/2 years later at the age of 35, we were able to walk away from our jobs into a wonderful new life.

Ever since that day, Judy and I have been blessed to help a lot of people realize the "much more" of life through this wonderful business.

We found that our purpose in life was to believe in people more than they believed in themselves, until they could believe in themselves more.

JIM and JUDY HEAD

When I think about dreams, I think about hope. I mean the kind of hope that fuels your daily decisions, that motivates you to keep going or get going, for that matter. When I think about dreams in my own life, it has become very obvious that they have played a vital role in helping Matt and me accomplish what we have. I think about the decisions we've made in our lives, and every time I do, I truly believe we were only able to make them because of the big dream we had and the true hope that our dream gave us. There were times when we fell upon doubt, hard times, and disbelief, but the hope of the dream life got us back up and kept us going. Dreaming breathes life in the soul; that's what it did for us. So often I believe we are taught to spend 40-60 hours a week working to build someone else's dream, but in my heart of hearts, I always knew that wasn't going to work for me. I desperately wanted a life that would allow me to not only build my own dream, but ultimately live it out daily. I wish I could give everyone the courage to dream big, to dream a dream that gets them off the couch and onto the field of their future. I truly believe that God wants us to dream big. He wants us to believe that we truly can accomplish anything we set our minds to. So often, my prayer is to be available to be used by God. I want God to use me in ways beyond what I can even fathom. I believe that God is using me to elevate the dreams of those who are reading this. I am calling you to believe that you can dream bigger than ever before! Why spend your whole life talking about your dream for retirement, when you can build that dream right here and now? Don't play small. God can and will use you in a powerful way if you have the faith to take action! Dream BIG my friends!

MATT and BRILEY NGUYEN

For us the dream is the ultimate fuel for everything we do in our lives! We choose to live for legacy, impact, significance, and purpose; and it is the dream that drives us to get up in the morning and work to make a difference, not just make a living. Growing up we were both taught to strive toward goals, get good grades, achieve, and find things that we are good at and go after those things. There was nothing wrong with this encouragement and it created in each of us a burning desire to accomplish our goals, BUT our view of life became very narrow and selfish, focused only on the things WE wanted. As soon as we started getting around "dream doers" and people whose dreams involved a bigger picture of including others, we started working a mostly dormant dream muscle to help us fashion a life that expanded our reach.

Now, as we strive toward becoming the best versions of ourselves here on planet Earth, the dream is what keeps us productive, youthful, awake, alive, and optimistic about the future. James Allen said, "The dreamers are the saviors of the world." That's because as dreamers we can make the impossible possible. We are the innovators, pioneers, and risk-takers that make the future a reality and we aren't afraid to fail while trying. Our dreams have been planted in our hearts from a great big God. We know that without them we will perish and with them we will flourish beyond what we could think or ask.

TERRY and JEN BROWN

We all want passion in our life. We all want to feel energized. To feel passionate, to feel energized, you must first start with identifying what you're fighting for. Start by identifying the goals and dreams for your life. The aggressive pursuit of your goals, your purpose, and your dreams is what gives you the passion and gives you the energy in your life that you desire. Take the time to think about and identify the dreams of your life and the purpose of your life. Then aggressively pursue them and you will live with passion and energy, and you will live *beyond your dreams!!*

RANDY and RAYE LYNN JASMAN

Dreaming provides you hope for your future and makes you excited to wake up each day to pursue that dream. Without a dream, people settle for an average life and stop pushing themselves out of their comfort zone to accomplish more. Dreaming also allows your kids to see an example of always pursuing something greater, and they learn to never limit themselves as to what is possible.

KENNY TOMS

I believe dreams are given to us by God. Knowledge of who we are and what we are meant to do on this earth is the greatest dream we can possess. You only love once. Obstacles and opposition will most certainly be placed in your path that will test you and your dream. Achieving your dream will require massive courage. Remember you are not alone. Through the strength and belief of dreamers comes the power to bless the lives of many others.

Dare to dream big, my friend.

RICK L. MARSHALL

Very seldom does your dream happen when you think it will or say it will, but with being consistent, dreams can and will come true. It's not always on our time, but when it comes, it is the right time. Never disregard being around like-minded people; the association is a key to making this all a reality. Not to mention what this will do for your marriage and your family. You are planting seeds that will show through the generations. If right now you do not have anyone that believes in you, then you must believe in you. And before you know it, like attracts like and you will never be alone. So, when we entered this opportunity, in my wife's and my minds, it was game on. There were slow times, dead ends, and roadblocks, and that's where a dream makes the difference. Where we lived had a small population, and we learned that may be an obstacle for some, but not us. We started out with a hope and a dream and sold out to the vision and accomplished a level that not only us, but others have said, "How did you do it?" It was a dream backed by action when we hit a level called EDC. Now take in every moment and be the dreamer that you know you are.

Blessings to you.

GATOR STRONG

A dream gives us hope and a vision for the future, and without it, life becomes empty. A dream, especially in this business, gives us purpose, joy, and satisfaction as we progress. It gives us the opportunity to make a difference in the lives of others.

HAL GOLDEN

When we were first exposed to Amway and World Wide, Hal and I didn't realize a life like this was even possible. But we knew we wanted more than an average, "just pay the bills" life. As we grew personally, worked hard, and built our business, our goals and dreams expanded. More and more choices became possible for our whole family with the rewards of investing in others. Achieving bigger goals and dreams hasn't always been easy for us, but it's always has been worth it!

ANN GOLDEN

In 1981, after working as a real estate broker for five years over 100 hours a week, Mary and I saw the Amway business. We weren't really excited about it even though we had the opportunity for a brand-new Diamond by the name of Dave Severn show us the plan in August of 1981. We were literally living the nightmare. Three years later after seeing another new Diamond get free, I finally caught the vision and went platinum that next year. The truth is, until we went Ruby, we couldn't even think about the dream; we could barely pay our bills.

Most young couples are living the nightmare. They've got a tiger by the tail and they can't stop; there's no time for a dream, they just need to get to the point where they can afford what they're already doing. That's where Ruby to Diamond came from; you've got to have a little space in your life before you can dream. Here's what most couples miss. The *foundation of a dream is hope* and that's where the dream gets lost.

So, what is hope? Let me define it this way. If today was the best day of the rest of your life and tomorrow got just a little worse and the next day got just a little worse and so on, how long would you want to live?

If today was the worst day of the rest of your life and tomorrow got just a little bit better and the next day got just a little bit better and so on, how long would you want to live.

The difference is hope; it's how you see the future and what its possibilities are.

So, for Mary and me, our dreams started when we could see a way forward, that by changing ourselves we could change our future. It's amazing what happens when you can pay your bills and have some left over.

God bless everyone,

DAVE and MARY TIMKO

Dreaming is the start to desiring change.

NAM DUKE KIM

In our opinion, to be a dreamer means to always have hope for the future. When there is hope in the future, there is power in the present. Being a dreamer means to believe in people's abilities to move forward and to believe that God has a plan for every single one of us. Dreaming is an action word, meaning we are always forward thinking. Dreaming is believing that we can always be and accomplish anything we want if we are willing to commit.

MAIKO and KULIA TUITUPOU

Dreams give you a reason for getting up in the morning. They put a bounce in your step and joy in your heart. Dreams usually stir your emotions to where you'll weep wanting them so bad.

Accomplishing dreams require an investment of time, encouraging association and the willingness to leave childish things behind.

NORM and PAM KIZIRIAN

We all have a God-given dream in our heart. Ignoring that dream leads to complacency. Acting on that dream leads to a life of adventure and forward motion. When we are in motion, we experience resistance. Resistance develops strength and emotional stability. Most importantly, resistance develops character. As we pursue the dream, it is not so much what we get as much as it is what we become through the ongoing process.

RANDY and SANDY SEARS *PERSON GROWTH*

What it means to dream: It means to hope and desire with a belief that the God-breathed vision to accomplish more is real. It means to live life to the fullest and know it can and will happen. It gives you the fuel to get after it every day until that dream comes to fruition.

SHANE and JOEY YADO

I always had a strong work ethic. But that was never enough in building a network business. Then one day, in two minutes, everything changed. A picture of the future (a dream) flashed in my heart while driving home on I-405 in San Diego. It is what we later called a God idea. I vividly described it to my wife and business partner, Leslie. We wept and we knew. One thousand days later, the picture manifested into reality. As in my dream, nearly 2,000 people in 25 states joined us at our conference, just like I saw it. I didn't work any harder. Instead, I had a dream embedded in my heart that was magnetic in moving us forward.

Dreamers are almost always misunderstood. But for us, it's the most treasured badge to be a dream builder.

Ross and Leslie Hall

My dreams were both huge and encouraged. They were a good start for our future. God began to challenge our hearts and we were captivated by our dreams to make room for what He had for us. He asked, "Are you comfortable with your dreams or are you willing to see what I can do with it?" Our big but limited dreams began to be replaced with a God-sized vision to impact others in bringing life, impact, and hope. He showed us a life I didn't even know to dream for. Our dreams are fulfilled while pursuing our God-sized life vision.

Andrea Phillips

My background on dreaming, like most people, was limited due to my past associations. But relationships with people who lived lives of fighting for their dreams, opened up in my late twenties. I started putting some reps in building new dreams that were uncomfortable for me. They gave me a new hop, skip, and jump in my walk. There is power in understanding how people sharing experiences of their God-size vision gives hope for all. This changed my mindset about my responsibility of dreaming big.

Kevin Phillips

We believe that a dream, a goal, and aspiring to something more is what keeps life fun and exciting. The Bible says that a man without a dream shall perish. This doesn't mean that you physically die, it means that one is perishing inside, in your soul. When you aim at nothing, you will hit nothing. When you are bored due to that lack of a dream, this leads to nonproductive habits at best.

We are so blessed in our great World Wide organization because we have an association of people who continue to strive to not only have more, but to impact more by becoming a better version of ourselves. As we grow the man or woman in the mirror, we naturally inspire others that they can do the same and create a worthy legacy.

Before you can achieve, you need to believe. Most of us heard this before but before you can believe, you need to want to believe. Some simply don't want to believe because of past life experiences or because it's just easier not to. I encourage you to change mental direction right now. What are you going to do with this most precious period of your life? What are you going to do with this year? What do you want to do, have, or become over the near future? Set a goal and get around the right people who encourage and help you to accomplish your dreams. Change habits and your life will radically change.

With God on your side, you can do it!

In His love,

SCOTT and CRIS HARIMOTO

It's interesting how we are often attracted to and fascinated by big dreamers. We're fascinated by what they have accomplished and continue to work on. We might think that their vision is a bit crazy or unrealistic, but deep down, we're rooting for their success. I believe in each of us there is a big dreamer waiting to be unleashed. However, when we dare to dream, those around us question and criticize our vision. How many of us have heard from those who love us, "be realistic"? Or, "that's just a pipe dream," or even, "nobody succeeds in that." We have found that learning to dream begins with a small seed of hope, the possibility that something can be. In order to grow this seed, we need to develop the muscle of dreaming, and the best way to develop this muscle is to get around those who dream big too! Like a trainer can help someone get into shape, learning from those who think hugely can help us learn and expand our own thinking. And just like how we need to remove weeds that might crowd out the healthy growth of a plant, we need to learn to remove our own limitations. We find a way. We start learning how to get around the challenge, through the challenge, or above the challenge. In the end, the dreams that are given to us are a responsibility, because they have the possibility to change our own world, the world around us, and maybe even the whole world itself.

Jon and Jen Rosario

Hi, we are Ty and Venessa Crandell. When Paul asked us to share our hearts and thoughts for his newest upcoming reading resource, we were so honored and thrilled! Paul has been an incredible blessing to us, and an instrument of hope, belief, strength, and an incredible solace for our family, our team and our personal and spiritual growth. Paul, you are simply amazing, and most of all, you are what John Maxwell would call "unforgettable."

We are where we are today in life because of all the amazing mentorship that has shaped us through our incredible lifeline and coaches and our World Wide Dream Builder System. We have always been dreamers, but today we realize more than ever the importance of having a dream.

We have come to understand that life is unfulfilling unless you have truly meaningful relationships to share, a dream for yourself and others, and people to love. We have been able to reshape the way we think about dreams and dreaming to include relationships, association, character building, and rewards.

We are so grateful to adapt the mindset that if you help others advance in life, you will ascend as well. We are excited to spend our life paying forward what we have been entrusted with.

TY and VENESSA CRANDELL

When I look back at my life of eighty-plus years, I realize that I didn't dream big enough. Most people think a dreamer is someone who thinks about things that are not possible or attainable. When you counsel with a World Wide Diamond, you will be told if your dream is realistic. They can show you how and why it's practical, and how it could be even bigger. With their coaching, you will learn how you can achieve it. If you listen, believe, and put in the work, your dream will come true.

ROGER and JOYCE FIX

ABOUT THE AUTHOR

Paul and Billie Kaye Tsika have been involved in ministry for more than forty-five years. He has authored several books including: *What You Seed Is What You Get, Sequoia-Size Success, Releasing Your Full Potential, The Overcomer's Edge*, and *The Language of Leadership*. Together they have authored books including: *Growing in Favor; Get Married, Stay Married;* and *Parenting with Purpose*. Paul has been the pastor of a large international marketing business since 2001. Along with their staff, they minister to tens of thousands of people each year and witness many coming to Christ for salvation. They reside at Restoration Ranch in Texas.

OTHER DESTINY IMAGE BOOKS BY PAUL TSIKA

The Overcomer's Edge: Strategies for Victorious Living in 13 Key Areas of Life

Growing in Grace: Daily Devotions for Hungry Hearts

OTHER DESTINY IMAGE BOOKS BY PAUL TSIKA AND BILLIE KAYE TSIKA

Parenting with Purpose: Winning the Heart of Your Child

Get Married, Stay Married

OTHER DESTINY IMAGE BOOKS BY BILLIE KAYE TSIKA

Priceless: A Woman of Strength